befor

WRITING A NOVEL

The Essential Guide

Samantha Pearce

Writing A Novel: The Essential Guide is also available in accessible formats for people with any degree of visual impairment. The large print edition and e-book (with accessibility features enabled) are available from Need2Know. Please let us know if there are any special features you require and we will do our best to accommodate your needs.

First published in Great Britain in 2012 by
Need2Know
Remus House
Coltsfoot Drive
Peterborough
PE2 9BF
Telephone 01733 898103
Fax 01733 313524
www.need2knowbooks.co.uk

Contents

Introduction

Embarking on the journey of novel writing is thrilling, exciting and, for many, an overwhelming passion. So much joy can be taken from creating characters from scratch, building lives for imaginary individuals who only exist in your head, and then on paper, in their own little stage show that hopefully others will go on and love. Abounds of pleasure can be sought from story-boarding an ingenious plot line, from finding just the right word to describe the street where your leading star resides, from realising that you can actually see the characters you have created from concept, as they have now become so vivid on paper. I sometimes think that there is nothing more rewarding than writing that final sentence and completing your very own delightful novel.

The purpose of this book

Writing a Novel – The Essential Guide is an interactive reference book that helps you create your own fiction masterpiece in a step-by-step, digestible way. This book is referred to as 'interactive' because it encourages the reader to participate in specific activities throughout each chapter which practically support the development of their novel. Each chapter contains a mixture of checklists, reflection points, templates and visual aids to guide the reader through each of the different elements of novel writing. At the end of each chapter you'll find a summary of the key points covered within the chapter, which can act as a reference guide for those readers who want to dip in and out of the book, and can also provide a handy refresh of the content covered.

Who is this book for?

This book has been written to support anyone and everyone who is interested in fiction writing. It is primarily intended for individuals who want to write their own novel, but also acts as a handy reference guide for anyone studying the art of novel writing, or who has an interest in how fiction works.

How will this book help me write my very own novel?

The content contained in this book is split into 11 comprehensive yet accessible chapters. Each chapter contains a number of headings and subheadings to guide you through the content in an easy and logical way. As you work your way through this book you'll find information, instructions and resources to help you complete each aspect of novel writing including:

- Learning what makes a good novel.
- Creating a writing schedule that works for you.
- Understanding the different genres of fiction.
- Structuring your novel.
- Assigning a plot and creating subplots.
- Developing characters.
- Learning how to make diction flow.
- Thinking about who will narrate your novel.
- Using language to create beautiful description.
- Reviewing, rewriting and editing.
- Deciding upon a publication route.
- Approaching publishers.

As with all of the reference books in the Need2Know series, *Writing a Novel – The Essential Guide* also includes a help list at the end of the book to signpost you on to other resources that can assist you in your novel writing, and to provide a fruitful source of reference.

Overall, it is hoped that this book provides you with the confidence and motivation to fulfil your dream of writing your very own novel, and what an achievement that is.

Chapter One

What is Fiction?

So you've decided that you want to write a novel. That's fantastic news. Writing a novel is one of those aspirations in life that many people hold, and few are motivated to pursue. The mere fact that you are reading this book demonstrates your commitment to fulfilling that ambition of creating a full work of fiction, regardless of whether your overarching aim is to have your novel published professionally, or whether you want to share your story informally with friends and family.

Having a desire to write a novel means by default that you wish to add to the vast library of varied and inspiring fiction works that are available throughout the world. Fiction is a fantastic field of writing to contribute to. It incorporates so many genres of writing and allows you to push your creative tendencies and stretch your ability to create individuals, relationships, environments and adventures. So much life can be born through successful, creative, fictional worlds. What then is meant by the term 'fiction'?

There are many definitions of fiction out there. Ultimately though, they all come to the same conclusion: 'Fiction is the form of any narrative or informative work that deals, in part or in whole, with information or events that are not factual' (en.wikipedia.org). Let's take a look at some of the most comprehensive definitions of fiction:

'(a) An imaginative creation or a pretence that does not represent actuality but has been invented. (b) The act of inventing such a creation or pretence. (c) A literary work whose content is produced by the imagination and is not necessarily based on fact. (d) The category of literature comprising works of this kind, including novels and short stories' (*www.thefreedictionary.com*).

'(a) The act of feigning, inventing, or imagining; as by a mere fiction of the mind. (b) That which is feigned, invented or imagined; especially a feigned or invented story, whether oral or written. (c) Fictitious literature; comprehensively,

'Writing a novel is one of those aspirations in life that many people hold, and few are motivated to pursue.'

all works of imagination; specifically novels and romances. (d) An assumption of a possible thing as fact, irrespective of the question of its truth' (*Webster Dictionary 2011*).

From these definitions we can identify that the most important element that must exist for a work to be considered as fiction is that:

The work should be created or invented through imagination, and therefore should not solely be based on fact.

To write a piece of fiction, the creation of an imaginary environment, populated by at least some invented characters or beings, is therefore required.

Why are people driven to write fiction?

It is difficult to know exactly how many fiction writers there are out there; even a count of published writers is, these days, almost impossible to undertake. Figures from sources such as R.R. Bowker, publishers of book industry statistics, can give us the number of US fiction books published that have been written in the English language, and we can then also look at the fiction publishing statistics for some of the larger UK book publishers, if we want to see what the UK writing market is looking like. To obtain a global picture however, we'd need to investigate the publishing figures for Australia, Canada, China, etc., and even then we'd still only be covering countries that publish fiction written in the English language.

It is safe to say that the number of fiction titles published each year is significant, and the ballpark number suggested in 2010 was that there are 100,000 new English-language works of long-form prose fiction published globally each year. That's a lot of books; generated by a lot of writers.

Why then are so many people motivated to write fiction? There are a number of reasons that drive people to create fictional pieces of writing. When looking to become a novel writer yourself, it can be useful to understand where your own motivation for writing springs from. Take a look at the list on the next page – it outlines some of the most common motivating factors for pursuing a fiction writing project – do any of these reasons reflect your own motivation for writing a novel?

Reasons for writing fiction	Does this reason motivate or influence my writing? (X as appropriate)
To entertain others	
To entertain ourselves	
To challenge ourselves	
To generate feelings in others. To enchant, inspire, be emotive and create empathy	
To tackle issues that are important to us, but to do so in a more creative way than simply using non-fiction research	
To explore the 'what ifs' in life	
To use the creative part of our mind	
To feel as if we have accomplished something	
To earn money	

Of course the list above is not exhaustive, and there will be many more personal reasons for writing fiction that are applicable on an individual basis. Take some time to think about these additional reasons for wanting to write a novel, as finding your motivational sources can be important when time, frustration and writer's block all start to take their toll. In addition, some writers find it useful to write a list of their reasons for wanting to write a book and to stick this list of reasons somewhere that is viewed often, perhaps on the fridge or above their computer, so that they can remain inspired even when the writing process itself becomes a little challenging.

Different types of fiction

It is widely recognised that there are two main types of fiction: literary and commercial.

'It is widely recognised that there are two main types of fiction: literary and commercial.'

Commercial fiction

Commercial fiction generally attracts a broad audience of readers, and books that are written as commercial fiction can fall into any subgenre, such as mystery, romance, legal thriller, Western, science fiction, and so forth. Some well-known 'blockbuster' commercial fiction authors include John Grisham, Sidney Sheldon, Danielle Steele and Jackie Collins.

Literary fiction

Literary fiction, on the other hand, tends to appeal to a smaller, more intellectually adventurous audience (*www.dummies.com*). Whilst a work of literary fiction can also fall into any subgenre of fiction, what sets literary fiction apart from commercial fiction are the notable qualities of writing style, originality and style that the book contains. Popular authors of literary fiction include Toni Morrison, Barbara Kingsolver, John le Carre and Saul Bellow.

Mainstream fiction

The term 'mainstream fiction' is a general term publishers and booksellers use to describe both commercial and literary works that depict a daily reality familiar to most people. These books, normally set in the 20th or present-day 21st century, have at their core a universal theme that attracts a broad audience (*www.dummies.com*). Mainstream books deal with topics such as family issues, coming of age initiations, courtroom dramas, career matters, physical and mental disabilities, social pressures, political intrigue, etc.

Alongside mainstream fiction, there are a number of more narrowly defined categories of fiction that are classified as genres or subgenres of fiction. These categories put novels into groups that are based on the subject matter of the book, i.e. mystery, romance or thriller. The table below outlines the principle genres of fiction.

Genre/ subgenre of fiction	Genre qualities	Example author(s)
Mystery	Mystery novels focus on a crime, usually murder. Subgenres include spy, detective and crime stories.	Arthur Conan Doyle, Raymond Chandler, Dashiell Hammett, Earle Stanley Gardner, Carl Hiaason, James Ellroy, Robert Parker, James Lee Burke, and Elmore Leonard.
Romance	Romance novels are generally aimed at a female readership. Romance novels normally incorporate key elements of other genres such as fantasy, love and adventure. Subgenres include historical, contemporary, fantasy romance and romantic suspense.	Jude Deveraux, Victoria Holt, Judith McNaught, Daphne Du Maurier, Jennifer Greene, and Nora Roberts.
Women's fiction	Women's fiction focuses on relationships, female protagonists, strong women, and unified women.	Barbara Taylor Bradford, Anne Rivers Siddons, Alice McDermott, Judith Krantz, Anne Tyler, Rebecca Wells, and Alice Hoffman.

Need2Know

Genre/ subgenre of fiction	Genre qualities	Example author(s)
Science fiction/ Fantasy	Science fiction/fantasy novels look at futuristic worlds which, whilst far removed from today's world, normally provoke contemplation of relevant issues affecting lives today.	Ray Bradbury, Arthur Clarke, Isaac Asimov, C.S. Lewis, R.R. Tolkien, and J.K. Rowling.
Suspense/ Thriller	Suspense novels and thrillers are often fast-paced, tense and exciting. Subgenres include political thrillers, military thrillers and courtroom thrillers.	John le Carre, Len Deighton, Ian Fleming, Clive Cussler, Frederick Forsythe, Patricia Cornwell, Tony Hillerman, Lawrence Sanders, Scott Turow, Richard North Patterson, Steve Martini, John Grisham, Tom Clancy and Stephen Koontz.
Western	Western novels are based on life in America's post Civil War Western frontier. They therefore normally involve conflicts between cowboys and outlaws, Native Americans, Easterners or Westerners.	Zane Grey and Louis Lamour.

Genre/ subgenre of fiction	Genre qualities	Example author(s)
Horror	Horror novels have one principle objective: to frighten readers by exploiting their fears.	Stephen King, Mary Shelley, Clive Barker, Peter Straub, Dean Koontz and Anne Rice.
Young adult	Young adult novels are led by a protagonist who is generally aged between 12 and 16 years.	J.K. Rowling, J.D. Salinger, Judy Blume and Louis Sachar.

It is important to consider what genre or subgenre of writing your novel will fall into, as this will ensure that you keep your writing focused on the principles of writing novels for this specific genre. A mystery novel, for example, must ensure that the outcome of the mystery is clearly conveyed to the reader at the end of the book. Similarly, romance novels must ensure that the outcome of the principle relationship followed throughout the book is satisfactory and 'real' for the reader; the outcome must match the twisted path of the relationship that the reader has followed throughout the novel, regardless of whether that outcome is positive or negative.

Examples of good fiction

There are so many examples of strong fiction out there! In order to write a good novel it is important to read novels that have been well written, and that fall into the same genre of fiction writing that you've chosen to pursue. The previous table should prove helpful here, for it identifies successful writers for each of the key genres of fiction writing. Before and during your personal novel-writing journey, take some time to read books that have been written by these published writers; you'll be amazed by how much you learn from absorbing their approach to characterisation, description, style, flow, diction and language.

To kick-start your exploration into some of the great writers of fiction, listed below are some wonderful examples of stories that manage to successfully combine, through fiction, both the delivery of entertainment with meaning. Use these writers as an informative source to help you strengthen your novel-writing craft.

- *Pride and Prejudice* by Jane Austin (1813).
- *The Tell-Tale Heart* by Edgar Allan Poe (1843).
- *The Adventures of Huckleberry Finn* by Mark Twain (1884).
- *The Lady with the Dog* by Anton Chekhov (1899).
- *The Great Gatsby* by F. Scott Fitzgerald (1925).
- *A Good Man is Hard to Find* by Flannery O'Connor (1955).
- *One Hundred Years of Solitude* by Gabriel García Márquez (1967).
- *The Things They Carried* by Tim O'Brien (1990).

The fundamentals of fiction writing

Fiction writing takes time, energy and boundless enthusiasm, and motivation. It also involves a certain amount of skill and ability to use the key elements of writing in such a way that a logical, interesting and meaningful novel is ultimately created. Throughout this book we shall look at these key elements of writing, and will identify ways that will help you use these elements in a complementary way, thereby enhancing your fiction writing. However, in addition to this knowledge, to succeed in your novel-writing task you'll also need to ensure that you can display the following fundamentals of fiction writing:

1. You need an idea or two on which to build your story. As Alexander Steele suggests, 'Ideas are seeds from which the mimosa tree or watermelon or delphinium of a story will arise', (*Gotham Writers' Workshop: Writing Fiction, 2008*).

2. You won't always feel motivated to write. But you need to allocate routine writing time to ensure that you make steady progress with your novel.

'Fiction writing takes time, energy and boundless enthusiasm, and motivation.'

3. Remain committed to research. Read the writing of others, and use their work to support the development of your own writing style.

4. Practise writing. Writing is a skill and so practising and experimenting with fictional writing can only help improve your ability to use this skill successfully.

5. Believe in yourself. You can write this novel. And you will. And it will be great.

Summing Up

- Writing a piece of fiction involves creating a story or series of stories that are based on imaginative circumstances, individuals, and/or environments. Many people have a desire to write works of fiction or to produce a novel, and there are lots of reasons why writing a novel appeals to so many.

- When deciding to write a novel it is important to identify your own personal reasons for wanting to create a work of fiction, for these reasons will help keep you motivated as you commit your ideas to paper.

- Fiction writing spans a number of genres: mystery, romance, mainstream and women's fiction, science fiction, fantasy, thriller, Western, horror and young adult fiction. Be sure to identify which genre of fiction your novel will fall into to ensure that you are meeting the expectations of your potential readers.

- To succeed in your goal to write a novel it is important that you: read the work of other writers, identify some routine writing time, practise writing fiction as frequently as possible, and, most importantly, believe in yourself and your ability to write a strong novel that you can be proud of.

Chapter Two

Creating a Writing Schedule

The master timetable

The art of writing is often thought to be a wonderful pastime; something that individuals are inspired to do whenever they have a free moment. And often writers, in the professional sense, are admired and envied – how fantastic to have a job that allows you to spend all day writing, thinking, planning, researching and just generally behaving in a 'creative' way! If only it were always that simple. Yes it is true that writing professionally brings great joy to many and it is often viewed as a privilege that writers rarely forget. However, unfortunately, as with all jobs, holding a career in writing brings with it a need to write to deadline, no matter how inspired or creative you may or may not be feeling. This same pressure can be felt by novice writers too, who are desperate to finish their novel as quickly as possible.

This responsibility of delivery often scares writers and can feel like a huge burden as they try to push forward with their novel. So how do you marry up the need for creative inspiration to guide well-written work and the need to ultimately finish that book? One of the easiest ways to meet both requirements is to create a writing schedule that reflects your own personal commitments and writing habits. After all, no one knows how you work better than yourself!

Creating a writing schedule can seem at first to be an easy task – you simply work out the deadline for your book (which may of course be self-driven) and you then work back towards today's date. This allows you to establish exactly how many days, weeks or months you have to finish all of your research, drafting, writing and editing. You can then cut your tasks into manageable

'As with all jobs, holding a career in writing brings with it a need to write to deadline, no matter how inspired or creative you may or may not be feeling.'

chunks, depending on the time available to you. For example, if you have 20 weeks between now and your final deadline, and you have a book that is 10 chapters long to write, then you may decide to give yourself 3 weeks for researching and planning, 2 weeks for drafting, 10 weeks for writing (one per chapter) and then 5 weeks for editing and revising.

The above certainly describes the first few steps you should go through when pulling together a realistic writing schedule. By slotting your tasks into available days and weeks, you are setting yourself a whole number of internal deadlines that can then seem more manageable in terms of completion. However, to ensure that the writing schedule really can be delivered, you next need to think about your own personal commitments and your writing pattern. Are there any days or weeks when you know the amount of time you have available to write is limited? If so you need to ensure that your writing schedule reflects a dip in performance across this period. Then consider how you tend to write. Do you write better on weekdays or weekends? Do you find that it takes you a long time to plan and to edit, but that the actual writing elements of your project are normally delivered quickly? You need to think about your own personal writing habits and then tailor your schedule accordingly. Creating a writing schedule isn't therefore always as straightforward as it may initially sound.

This chapter looks at the thinking and planning process that you need to go through when creating a writing schedule that works for you.

Agreeing a deadline

In order to create a writing schedule, you first need to decide when you want to have your novel completed. This completion date needs to reflect all of the elements of finalising a novel; re-reading through the novel in its entirety, editing the novel as required and proofreading the manuscript to ensure that it is error-free.

Determining a deadline can be a daunting task as it is formally marking the completion date for the book that you are so carefully crafting. Working to a deadline can also be hugely motivational however, for it provides a focus and will help ensure a sense of purpose is added to each piece of writing that you undertake.

'Working to a deadline can be hugely motivational for it provides a focus and will help ensure a sense of purpose is added to each piece of writing that you undertake.'

Allocating a writing deadline requires some thinking! You'll need to take a number of factors into consideration before settling on a date. Below is a list of factors for you to consider when identifying your deadline. Work through each factor in turn and determine (a) if it is applicable to your personal circumstances, and (b) what impact this factor might have on the potential completion date for your novel:

- Have you secured interest in your book from a literary agent or publisher? If so, their preferred receipt date for the manuscript needs to be adhered to.

- Is the book being written for a particular event? For example, if you are writing the book as a birthday present for a loved one, you'll need to ensure that the book is completed and, if applicable, designed, printed and bound in time for the birthday date.

- Do you have any significant events scheduled in the short term that will dramatically reduce your writing time or ability? If so, consider how possible it is to complete the novel before this date, as taking a long break from novel writing can make it difficult to recommence the writing of the book at a later date.

- Are your work or home schedules/commitments about to peak? If so, how can you continue to manage writing time around these commitments without placing enormous stress on yourself?

- Do you find that you are a more productive writer at certain times of the year? If so, is it possible to schedule a deadline that maximises this preferred writing time?

Now that you've identified your ultimate production deadline, your next step is to determine your writing availability between now and this deadline. Now is the time to think logically about some of the factors outlined above; work commitments, family commitments and preferred writing periods.

Time availability

There's no 'average amount of time to write a novel' figure; hence the need to determine a deadline and supporting timetable that meets your personal requirements and time availability. However, for the purposes of this chapter, let's assume that you have a 100,000-word novel to write, and that you want to have the novel completed within 8 months. That gives you 32 weeks to plan, research, write and edit the novel. Initially you could split your time evenly as follows:

- 4 weeks for planning and completing required research.
- 3 weeks for proofreading and editing.
- That leaves you with 25 weeks to write the novel.
- 100,000 words/25 weeks = 4,000 words to be written per week.

For many writers, this will be an achievable target. 4,000 words of fiction can, if writer's block doesn't get in the way, be written in 4-8 hours and many writers find that they have the capacity to fit this protected time into their week. However, it might not be possible to fit it into every week available over the next 8 months. This is where expanding and collapsing time availability comes into play.

First, think about any events that might stop you meeting your 4,000-word deadline over a particular week or series of weeks. Examples of events include: planned peaks in your work life, family holidays or occasions, and scheduled health care.

Calculate how many writing weeks these events will disrupt. This will then allow you to calculate how many additional words you need to build into the rest of your writing time.

The next phase of your planning is to identify when and where you might be able to accommodate these extra words. To do this, look for times when you are either going to have more spare time to write, or where you might be more motivated to write.

Holidays can be a great time to complete some additional novel writing, as they provide you with hours in the day that are normally lost to working life. Even if you do have children, spouses or even animals to entertain during a holiday period, individuals often find that they have more spare time to complete creative writing when they are on holiday than they do at any other time in the year.

'Holidays can be a great time to complete some additional novel writing, as they provide you with hours in the day that are normally lost to working life.'

In addition, lots of writers find that they are more productive in the summer months; perhaps because nicer weather makes you 'feel' more energetic and creative anyway. Writers generally have more exposure to creative tasks in the summer too; baking, gardening, outdoor play with children, walking etc. – these are all activities that can be considered as creative and they are more prolifically embraced during the summer. The completion of one creative activity usually leads to the completion of another, and so successful creative writing is more likely to be completed throughout the summer months. Evenings are also lighter in the summer, so it can feel as if there is more free time for leisure activities to be undertaken.

The other period of time that is often quite conducive to creative writing is the Christmas period. The general feeling of goodwill and happiness that most experience over the Christmas period can leave writers energised and thus more productive in their work.

Setting realistic milestones

Once you have determined your deadline and the manner in which you are going to reach that deadline, i.e. how many words you are planning to write each week, your next step is to identify mini-deadlines or milestones that you can aim for on a reasonably frequent basis.

A milestone is an intermediate action that needs to be reached or made in order to ensure that you meet the ultimate objective of a project; in this case that ultimate objective is the completion of your novel. By setting intermediate goals or milestones, you can instil a sense of self-achievement at frequent points throughout the novel-writing process. Not only does this make the overarching task of writing a novel seem a little more achievable (for each time you're working towards a smaller goal as opposed to that overwhelming goal of producing an entire novel), but it is also hugely motivational as you can get a sense of achievement as each milestone is successfully met.

Everyone has a different approach to setting milestones. Some people set milestones based on how many words they've written; others use specific points of the storyline as markers for milestone success. It doesn't really matter

'By setting intermediate goals or milestones, you can instil a sense of self-achievement at frequent points throughout the novel-writing process.'

how you define your milestones, but what is important is that you acknowledge the attainment of them, and that you ensure that you have set sufficient milestones to keep you motivated throughout your writing journey.

Motivations to write

There are lots of great reasons to write a book, and as a budding novelist you've identified your own passion for creating a piece of fiction. Nonetheless, writing a book requires significant levels of motivation. It can feel like a task that won't be achieved, and one that you therefore don't necessarily know if you're strong enough to take on. But often the hardest hurdle to overcome is starting to commit your ideas to paper; once this has been achieved the rest of your novel generally tends to flow quite smoothly.

We all need support and motivation to start the daunting task of novel writing, however. So to help keep you inspired in your novel-writing journey, here are some great reasons as to why writing a book is most definitely a worthwhile experience:

Follow opportunities to visit new places and meet new people

Writing your book will no doubt give you the opportunity to visit new places, travel to new counties and (if you're lucky) to new countries. All very exciting! Whilst travelling can give you the opportunity to visit new places, it can also introduce you to people that you'd never normally interact with. Furthermore, by holding book launches, book signings and book readings, you'll get an opportunity to meet individuals from your local community that you may never have interacted with before.

You might just become famous!

OK, so it is very difficult to become an international celebrity, but by writing a number of books and working hard on the marketing and advertising of these books, it is possible to become something of a local celeb. Remember to share your experiences with as many people as possible, either through local talks and readings, or through interviews for the local press. Work with groups of people who are interested in writing and learn to motivate them too. All of this will not only make you feel good for giving something back to the community, it will also help boost your personal profile.

Make yourself, your friends and your family proud

Writing a book is a wonderful achievement, and one that should be celebrated. But once the party is over, once you've had that last round of drinks in celebration, keep hold of how immensely proud you feel of yourself, and know that those around you who love you also feel extremely proud of your achievement.

Flex your creative muscles

Creativity is of paramount importance to all novel writing. And creativity is one area of life that tends to get lost as you grow up and find that the practicalities of 'normal' day-to-day life take up too much of your time. But by writing a book you will find that you have the opportunity to claw back some of that creativity that is usually drained away through day-to-day life.

Kill off another of life's regrets

Most of us have things that we regret doing . . . and indeed not doing. Don't let not writing that book become another regret to add to your list. Lots of people regret never writing that book that is inside of them; I've never heard of anyone who actually regretted writing a book.

Create a new income stream

Published books can generate income for you that may previously have been unobtainable. Whilst it can take time and patience to build up sufficient readership to really reap the benefits of book writing, if you put into place a good marketing campaign and plan to write additional books, you may find that you can make book writing a lucrative income stream for you and your family.

Summing Up

- A writing timetable is an important tool that any novelist should look to utilise. It is important to create a timetable that meets your own personal needs, and that works to milestones and overarching deadlines that are realistic and achievable.

- Don't underestimate how draining the task of writing a novel can be, despite the fact that it is a hugely exciting project that should invoke an enormous sense of pride.

- Identify the reasons or actions that motivate you to write, and draw on these often as you continue to develop your novel.

Chapter Three

The Different
Genres of Fiction

In chapter 1 we outlined the different genres of fiction, looking briefly at some of the prevailing qualities of these genres and identifying some of the key and established writers of each genre in order to support your ongoing research into the particular area of writing within which your novel will sit.

In this chapter we will look in more detail at each of the dominant genres of fiction. This will provide you with a greater understanding of the key characteristics that exist in each of these genres and will therefore almost serve as a checklist for you, so you can ensure that your own writing style contains, at least in part, a number of these principle genre characteristics. Remember, originality is great, but no matter how unique a book may be, for it to be recognised and received by a reader it must allude to the much-loved characteristics of the genre that it's written for – well, at least a little!

Before you begin reading through this chapter, take some time to jot down what you already know about each of the different genres explored in this chapter. These genres will be:

- Mainstream fiction (contemporary).
- Mystery.
- Romance.
- Science fiction/fantasy.
- Horror.
- Young adult.

Use the following questions to help shape the completion of this task:

1. What is the target audience for a book that falls into each of the previous genres?

2. How can you determine that a book falls into each of the genres listed?

3. What characteristics do the main characters of books from each of the genres display?

4. What would you say is the conventional form for books contained within each of the genres listed previously?

5. What sort of writing style is dominant across books found in each of the genres outlined previously?

Mainstream fiction

Mainstream fiction is a funny little genre, in so far as novels that fall into this category tend not to abide by any of the typical conventions of other genres. In this way, mainstream fiction is a very wide genre, covering a range of subject areas, focuses and novel characteristics. Basically, if a novel doesn't fit into any of the more specific genres, and you wouldn't refer to it as a literary book (see chapter 1), then it is likely to be classified as a piece of mainstream fiction.

When speaking to aspiring writers (survey conducted by Words Worth Reading Ltd, 2012 – www.wordsworthreading.co.uk), a number of useful definitions of mainstream fiction arose. These definitions help provide the principle elements of books that fall into the mainstream fiction genre:

'I define it as current fiction, set in a current time period, with everyday characters, doing everyday things'.

'A book that has a bit of everything in it. It doesn't concentrate on one specific genre. It has some adventure, love, fantasy, comedy and more. No one element overpowers the others'.

'Mainstream fiction to me is not genre consistent and isn't concerned with niche markets; instead it appeals to broader audiences and covers quite universal concepts, set in worlds that aren't drastically different to the one we inhabit'.

'Mainstream fiction focuses on plot'.

'Mainstream fiction refers to the stories that you want to vicariously live out yourself, hence its appeal to the mainstream'.

From the quotes above we learn about a number of the key characteristics that define mainstream fiction:

- The setting of mainstream fiction is normally within the current time period, and the world in which the story unfolds is the same (or very similar) to the world that we all live in today.

- Believability is crucial to the success of mainstream fiction. The reader must be able to (a) believe in the characters, (b) believe that the story that unfolds could happen, and (c) believe that the story that unfolds could indeed happen to them.

Mystery

The Penguin Group states that 'a mystery is a story that has five basic but important elements. These five components are: the characters, the setting, the plot, the problem, and the solution. These essential elements keep the story running smoothly and allow the clues to the solution of the mystery to be revealed in a logical way that the reader can follow'.

Let's look at each of these five elements in a little more detail:

- Characters – In a mystery novel the main character will determine the way the plot or mystery will develop. Furthermore, the main character is usually the person who will solve the problem that the story's mystery is centred upon. However, no mystery can be complete without secondary characters to provide clues to aid in the resolution of the problem, or indeed to hinder the resolution of the problem. With mystery novels there is often a wide range of secondary characters as this variety and level of intervention into the mystery adds intrigue to the story itself.

- Setting – More often than not, an everyday or familiar setting is used in mystery novels as this can help the reader feel greatly involved with the plot.

'Believability is crucial to the success of mainstream fiction.'

However, mystery novels have been set in fantasy environments before, and as long as the description of these environments is strong, the reader should still be able to connect with the plot line.

- Plot – A strong plot line is crucial to a mystery story, perhaps more so than in any other genre. For a mystery book to be intriguing to a reader, the reader must feel as if he or she is taking part in the resolution of the problem; they must feel connected to the plot. Furthermore, as the resolution of the mystery is identified, the reader must be able to look back over the plot and think, 'Yes! I can see how this solution has been determined.'

- Problem – Every mystery has a problem to solve, and often this problem is focused on a crime, who committed the crime and why.

- Solution – The solution to the problem is the way the action is resolved, the individual who committed the crime is identified for example. For a mystery book to be strong, it is important that the solution is believable and, in addition, it is important that the reader can determine how the solution came about, by reanalysing the plot line of the book.

Romance

The desire to write romantic fiction is very common and there are many people who want to pen the next *Gone With the Wind* or *Dr Zhivago*. However, writing romantic fiction is not easy and, as with all styles of writing, there are certain criteria that you need to follow. Mills and Boon stories may seem simple when you read them, but there is still a lot of work and preparation that goes into them.

If you do wish to write romantic fiction, one of the best ways of getting an idea about the genre, style and type of language used is to read other books. This way you can put together a picture and develop an awareness of the language used and start to build a background of the genre. By reading other romance novels you will get the feel of what works well and what doesn't so that you can use this knowledge in your writing. If you really want to get to know your craft you need to study it, so the more books you read the better. Think of it as studying for an exam, but far more enjoyable!

'By reading other romance novels you will get the feel of what works well and what doesn't so that you can use this knowledge in your writing.'

There are a number of key elements that need to be included in romance writing to make it strong and therefore more likely to be noticed by a publisher. These elements include:

- A good opening line – Most people tend to read the opening line and the back cover of a book before deciding to buy it, so the opening line needs to be strong and capture the reader from the off. 'Last night I dreamt I went to Maderley again . . . '

- Good punctuation and grammar – Often romance novels are read by female readers, and women are more likely to be put off a novel if they continue to find frustrating errors in the text. Whilst strong grammar and punctuation is crucial to all forms and genres of writing, for this reason it is particularly important when writing romance.

- Good dialogue – Each line has to ensure that the story is advanced, the connection between the hero/heroine is intensified and that any conflict between them is deepened.

- A compelling plot – In romance writing there is a need to ensure that the focus of the plot line remains on the relationship between the hero and the heroine, and on their emotions surrounding this romance. For this reason, it is often better to ensure a strong lead plot as opposed to introducing a number of subplots which can, at times, de-focus the reader.

- Subplots – As suggested in the point above, romantic stories do often incorporate subplots such a murder storyline or a medical storyline, but crucially they always maintain the underlying story of romance.

- Emotions – A focus on showing as opposed to telling the emotions of a character is always seen in romance fiction, for it is so important to establish a strong sense of personality for each of the principle characters within the book.

- Captivating scenes – Most examples of strong fiction writing work on a scene-building basis, with each scene leaving the reader wondering what will happen next. As one conflict is resolved, another more dramatic scene often appears, compelling the reader to find out how the hero or heroine will manage with the conflict or drama that is unfolding. Indeed, romantic novels often build conflict into their storylines which force the hero and heroine apart. This element of conflict creates reader intrigue.

- Strong characters – Characters are a principle element of all novels, and within romantic fiction particularly, it is important to (a) see characters grow throughout the book and (b) instil a level of empathy and care for the characters within the book's readers.

- Sexual tension – No book could be classified as falling into the romance genre if it didn't ensure that a level of sexual tension was built up between the hero and heroine.

- A happy ending – In the majority of romantic fiction, the outcome of the story is positive, and one that the reader will have been rooting for as they read their way through the book.

Fantasy

'Fantasy writing can be an awful lot of fun!'

Fantasy writing can be an awful lot of fun! It is one of the genres of writing that allows you to really let your imagination run wild, in a way that standard fiction writing often doesn't allow you to do. Horror writing sits, to some extent, within the same realm as fantasy writing in so far as it allows the writer to be particularly creative with the plot line, but the genre of fantasy allows writers to create entire new worlds, universes and ways of living. This is something that other genres of writing just can't compete with.

If you find yourself compelled to write a fantasy book, remember that writing within the fantasy genre does not allow you to escape from the standard yet crucial elements of novel writing. These core elements include:

- Well-developed and believable characters.

- One (or potentially two) lead heroes or heroines that are easily identifiable throughout the book.

- A mixture of direct speech and narration.

However, there are also key features of successful fantasy writing that are distinct from other forms of novel writing. These key features are:

- Fantasy stories need to have a clear structure, and generally this structure will take the lead character, and thus the reader, from the 'normal' world, across or through into a fantasy world, and then back into everyday, normal life again. It may be that this pattern is repeated throughout the book, but often fantasy writers will simply stick to this three-world-move structure.

- As stated previously, fantasy stories should have a hero or a heroine. In fantasy writing we see the hero or heroine undergoing a number of experiences throughout the day which lead to some form of lasting character transformation. This transformation could be physical or emotional.

- Overall a fiction novel will convey some form of 'learning point' – a lesson that the reader can take away from the book. Generally this learning point is communicated through the lead character.

- And finally, no matter how creative the places and characters may be within a fiction story, in successful fiction writing they always remain believable within the boundaries of the story. Consistency is of paramount importance when it comes to fantasy writing.

Horror

The range of stories that can be covered in horror fiction is vast; perhaps much wider than many initially think. Images of Shelley's *Frankenstein* often come immediately to mind when the notion of writing horror fiction is first pondered, but nowadays horror fiction is much wider than stories that focus on ghosts and ghouls.

Webster's Collegiate Dictionary defines horror as, 'a painful and intense fear, dread, or dismay'. It thus stands to reason that 'horror fiction' is fiction that elicits these emotions in the reader. So, what makes good horror fiction? Let's look at five crucial elements:

1. Suspense – Horror fiction has to have some element of suspense. Furthermore, that suspense must be build on an action or event that would horrify a contemporary audience, and that might not be blood, guts and gore. A series of killings that the police can't fathom, however, just might work.

2. The 'cover your eyes' moment – This is so much easier to achieve on screen, but needs to be captured in horror novels too. Think back to successful horror films where the viewer sees a character walk towards a room, trying to explore what is inside it, and all the while ominous background music is getting higher and higher in pitch and louder and louder in volume. Then suddenly . . . a thud which reveals something horrid or something silly. Either way, the audience are hiding behind their hands, scared to peek through their fingers. This level of anticipation needs to also be achieved through text.

3. Ghosts and villains – A horror novel needs a bad guy; someone or something that is inciting the horror. In the last century this would almost always have been a ghost of some description, but today's horror audience tend to look for more believable villains.

4. Murder – Incorporating murders into the plot line is an almost essential element of a horror novel. Generally, the more the merrier so to speak.

5. Believable characters – As we've seen for all genres (other than perhaps fantasy), characters in horror stories need to be believable. Even if a horror story has a number of supernatural beings featured within it, these supernatural beings tend to have human traits coupled with their antihuman nature which allows the reader to hold a real fear for the characters.

'Writing teenage fiction can be a wonderful way to reach young adults who often feel unsupported and lost in their quest to learn more about themselves.'

Young adult

The term 'young adult' when applied to fiction refers to any book that has been written for a teenage audience. Writing teenage fiction can be a wonderful way to reach young adults who often feel unsupported and lost in their quest to learn more about themselves. Many can see the real benefit in writing young adult fiction:

'There is almost nothing you can't tackle in a teenage novel' – Marcus Sedgwick.

'A young adult novel (to my mind) is essentially an adult novel that will appeal particularly to teenagers' – Garth Nix.

'Good Y.A. is like good television. There's a freshness there; it's engaging. Y.A. authors aren't writing about middle-aged anomie or disappointed people' – GalleyCat.

'Let us celebrate the innovative fashion in which today's YA authors are bending the traditional definitions of genre' – Scott Smith.

With young adult fiction, essentially the elements of the novel are the same as those elements that dominate adult fiction, split out into the many genres of fiction writing in general. However the voice seen in young adult fiction differs to that found in adult fiction, and the mindset of the narrator is different. In addition, the language used in teen fiction reflect the quirks of contemporary teen language at the time of writing the novel, so phenomenons such as 'text speak' are generally incorporated.

The key elements of young adult fiction include:

- A youthful narrative voice – Teen fiction or young adult fiction is narrated by a character of this age, somewhere between 12 and 18. This can be difficult to achieve for authors who don't themselves fall within this age bracket. Successful young adult fiction writers ensure that they adopt a relaxed tone of speech which doesn't always stick to the rules of grammar, never preaches, embraces drama and always demonstrates a youthful level of immaturity.

- A heavy use of dialogue – Teen fiction focuses on speech as opposed to description. Speech is fluid, simple and full of relaxed syntax.

- Dramatic – Often the events in young adult fiction reflect everyday teenage life, but the manner in which they are told is dramatic, reflecting the way in which the readers view their own life at that given point in time.

Summing Up

- As emphasised in chapter 1, understanding the genre for which you are writing your novel is crucial to the overall success of the novel itself. In this chapter we have explored in detail the characteristics of some of the principle genres found in fiction writing.

- Mainstream fiction deals with contemporary issues in a contemporary setting and is plot-focused.

- Mystery fiction focuses on a complicated plot line which ultimately leads the reader to resolve the mystery that is at the core of the story.

- Romantic fiction must keep the principle romantic story at the core of the book and must provide the readers with a happy and almost unsurprising conclusion.

- Fantasy writing allows the reader to enter a new realm, world or universe. However it is important that the world is still believable and therefore approachable to readers.

- No matter how many ghosts, ghouls and murders you include in horror fiction, ultimately the plot line and characters must be believable to allow the reader to feel the much needed suspense and fear.

- Young adult fiction looks at teenage and adult issues from a teenage point of view. Language is diction-driven and dramatic, with the narrator almost always a teenager themselves.

Chapter Four

Fiction Structure

All writing, whether fictional or non-fictional, needs to have some form of structure. Think about any piece of writing that you've read recently and you'll quite quickly be able to see that it follows a fairly standardised structure; there is a beginning or introduction, there is the middle, and then there is the ending. This structure can be applied to almost any piece of written communication including:

- Novels.

- Short stories.

- Factual writing.

- Novellas.

- Articles.

- Blog posts.

- Letters.

- Press releases.

- Marketing material such as brochures or leaflets.

This writing structure has existed for more than 23 hundred years, since Aristotle wrote his piece titled *Poetics*, and continues to be trusted by authors today as a foolproof way to organise a novel.

The structure of a novel links closely to the plot of a novel; the two are intertwined. Whilst the plot provides a way to organise the story that you are writing, the structure provides a way to keep the sequence of events that happen in the book in a strong and 'good' order. We'll look at how plot and book structure meet in the next chapter, but for now, let's focus on the three key elements of a book's structure; the beginning, the middle and the end.

'The structure of a novel links closely to the plot of a novel; the two are intertwined.'

The beginning

Ultimately, the opening to a novel, or the novel's beginning, has three main aims:

1. Capture the reader's attention. It fulfils this aim by dropping the reader right into the middle of the action or drama.

2. Provide all of the background information the reader needs to be able to (a) understand the significance of the plot and (b) form a bond with the lead characters.

3. Identify for the reader the significant event or challenge that is going to dominate the plot line.

The following table outlines in more detail how the beginning of a novel can go about fulfilling these aims.

The aims of the beginning of a novel	How a novel fulfils these aims	Thinking points
Capture the reader's attention. It fulfils this aim by dropping the reader right into the middle of the action or drama.	There is no point starting a book days before any of the action starts. Don't start the book when life is ticking along as normal, start at the point of change. Providing a précis of the personality and background stories of lead characters or describing the setting of your story are most definitely not ways to capture the reader's attention from the start.	Imagine you were telling your friend a story about something really exciting that'd happened. You wouldn't start your storytelling days before the event, you'd start in the thick of the excitement. The same is true in story writing – don't start the story in advance of the exciting event – get straight in there and worry about the background information later. Often a dramatic opening sentence or paragraph that places the reader right in the thick of the story is the best way to fulfil this aim. Brainstorm dramatic sentences or paragraphs that would fulfil this aim for you.

The aims of the beginning of a novel	How a novel fulfils these aims	Thinking points
Provide all of the background information the reader needs to be able to (a) understand the significance of the plot and (b) form a bond with the lead characters.	It may seem as if this aim contradicts the previous one, but the two need to work in harmony with one another for the beginning of a book to 'work'. Whilst the opening to a story needs to place the reader in the thick of the action, it also needs to provide the reader with sufficient information about the situation and the characters for the reader to be able to understand the events, and the characters' reactions to them. In order to balance out the provision of information to the reader with the need to captivate the reader by placing them straight in the action, an author needs to expose only the background information that the reader needs at a given point in time – no more.	Balancing the need to captivate with the need to expose background information to the reader is a skill that requires practice, trial and error, and research. Look at how other authors achieve this balance to help you master this skill yourself. Remember that information should be provided on a need-to-know basis only, and that the way in which the information is presented to the reader should be interesting, relevant, and integrated with the action that is unfolding across the opening scenes.

Need2Know

The aims of the beginning of a novel	How a novel fulfils these aims	Thinking points
Identify for the reader the significant event or challenge that is going to dominate the plotline.	This aim is generally achieved by providing the standpoints or situations of the lead characters and indicating where a challenge or conflict might lie. We might, for example, learn that Pippa has been trying to have a baby for several years now and that this is taking a toll on her emotional wellbeing, especially as her husband is happy to accept a future without children and she really isn't. Or we could see the formation of two gangs, with a brief understanding of why they dislike each other so strongly. At this point we don't need to know any more, only that the story is going to focus on this overarching challenge.	The key here is to let the reader have a sense of what the main challenge or significant event in the book is going to be, without dwelling on it too much – after all you still have the middle and ending of the book to create!

'The opening to a novel has a very important role – captivating the reader, giving some background and context to the story, and showing the reader where the story is heading.'

All three of the aims of the beginning of a novel are challenging to deliver, particularly as they have to be delivered in such a way that they harmonise with each other. It is clear that the opening to a novel has a very important role – captivating the reader, giving some background and context to the story, and showing the reader where the story is heading – however despite this, the beginning of a novel is typically very short. After all, the reader is keen to move on to the middle of the book where the real action starts to unravel, and so the beginning of a novel needs to fulfil its objectives and then hand over to 'the middle'.

The middle

The middle section of a novel and the beginning or opening of a novel will overlap a little; the story just wouldn't flow if they didn't. However there are some key characteristics to the middle of a book that should be recognised and then utilised when writing a novel:

'The focus of the story, whether this be a challenge that needs to be overcome or a problem that seeks resolution, is played out in the middle of a book.'

- The middle of a story takes up the majority of space in a book – it represents far more words than either the beginning or the ending of the novel.

- Most of the story is developed and presented within the middle section. It is here that the reader will find (a) the majority of exposition to the situation and the characters' lives, personalities and relationships, and (b) the delivery of the prominent events that make up the plot line and any subplots.

- The focus of the story, whether this be a challenge that needs to be overcome or a problem that seeks resolution, is played out in the middle of a book. Here the reader often sees the tension of the novel increase and increase until it can grow no further. It is important, however, that the tension of the novel is based upon the key challenge or event that was exposed to the reader in the beginning of the novel.

- A strong sense of order dominates the middle of a novel. The reader learns more about the characters, and the plot lines are developed in this section of the book, but this development of the story and of the reader's knowledge is completed in a logical and ordered manner.

The end

Often the ending of a novel is the shortest part of the book. This does not mean, however, that it is any less important or significant than the beginning and middle of the story.

The ending of a story is generally dominated by what's often referred to as 'the three Cs' – crisis, climax and consequences. Ebenbach (*Gotham Writers' Workshop: Writing Fiction, 2008*) defines these three Cs nicely: 'The crisis is the point where tension hits its maximum, and the climax is where the tension breaks, and where we get our answer to our major dramatic question. Then, the consequences, however briefly handled, are alluded to at the very end of the piece'.

The ending of a novel then provides an answer to the question the novel has been striving to answer or a resolution to the challenge that the lead characters in the book have been working to overcome. The reader sees that last hurdle tackled and (generally) successfully overcome. To close the novel the reader then gets a glimpse of what life will be like for the lead characters now that this episode in their life is over. And this glimpse into the future represents the consequences of the events that have taken place throughout the novel.

Chronology

Within the structure of a novel, and particularly within the middle part of a book, it is important that a consistent chronology of events is in place. This doesn't mean that as an author you cannot flick between time periods, after all lots of novels include a mixture of present tense scenes and those that have taken place in the past. However the overall order in which events took place or take place needs to remain consistent.

Perhaps the best way to ensure that events always remain in chronological order is to create a timeline for the events that will run through the novel in advance of committing the novel to paper. By following a timeline of events as you create your novel, you'll be able to guarantee that the plot(s) of your story make sense to the reader at all times. Not only does this add a sense of grounding for the reader, but it also makes your writing more reliable and thus much more 'real'.

'The ending of a novel then provides an answer to the question the novel has been striving to answer or a resolution to the challenge that the lead characters in the book have been working to overcome.'

Summing Up

- The structure of a novel is entwined with the plot of a novel; whilst the plot lays down the events that unfold throughout the book, the structure of a novel helps bring a sense of order to the book itself.

- The structure of a book is made up of three core elements: a beginning, a middle and an ending. Each element has its own function to complement the delivery of the story.

- The beginning of a novel is there to (a) captivate the reader by drawing them into the action of the story from the outset, (b) provide essential background information to the reader, and (c) identify the key challenge, problem or issue that the novel will deal with.

- The middle of a novel is where the majority of action is played out. Here the tension of the novel should increase until it can grow no further. In the middle of a novel the reader also learns more about the characters and sees the lead character or characters strive towards resolution of their challenge, problem or issue. The middle part of a novel represents the largest section of a book.

- The ending pulls the strands of the story together. Dominated by 'the three Cs' – crisis, climax and consequence – the ending lets the reader discover if and how the characters resolve their challenge, problem or issue. Furthermore, through the ending of the novel the readers get the opportunity to glance at how life will be for the characters now, moving forward.

- Finally, it is important that a consistent chronology of events is in place, particularly throughout the middle of the book. An author can achieve this by creating a timeline to adhere to throughout the writing process.

Chapter Five

Plot

So, when it comes to novel writing, what is plot? The plot is another word for the series of events that make up the storyline that runs through the novel. Or, as the dictionary defines it:

'Also called storyline; the plan, scheme, or main story of a literary or dramatic work, as a play, novel or short story' – dictionary.reference.com

'The pattern of events or main story in a narrative or drama' – www.thefreedictionary.com

The story that you are writing is therefore the plot of the novel.

Remember, this is fiction!

Fictional pieces of writing often reflect elements of real life. It is important to remember, however, that fiction only reflects some parts of real life, and these parts of life are then either magnified, enhanced or surrounded by creative plot lines to create a piece of fiction that's worth reading.

Real life in itself is generally quite mundane. As adults we wake, eat, clean, work, eat, relax and sleep – that's pretty much our routine day. And of course there are days or weeks or even longer periods of our life where this routine is taken over by something more exciting, challenging or upsetting, but once this event has past, normal life resumes and tends to rule.

Novels would be very dull if they focused on the day-to-day life of us humans. Readers do not generally want to see characters waking up, eating their breakfast, yelling at the kids to get out of bed, completing the school run, going off to work, avoiding the boss, racing to the shops during rush hour, cooking tea, helping children with their schoolwork, putting a load of washing

'Fiction only reflects some parts of real life, and these parts of life are then either magnified, enhanced or surrounded by creative plot lines to create a piece of fiction that's worth reading.'

on and finally heading to bed. This sequence of events they see in their own lives each day, and so reading about it offers no real form of entertainment or enjoyment.

That's not to say, however, that you as an author shouldn't understand the day-to-day routine of your characters. One of the biggest challenges that faces novel writers is the need to create 'real' characters – characters that are believable to the readers who follow their journey through your book. Part of the process for creating characters that are as 'real' as possible is to ensure that you, their creator, knows everything you possibly can about them. This includes understanding their daily life (see chapter 6). Obtaining this knowledge of their routine behaviours is therefore an important part of your planning and research process when it comes to novel writing. It does not, however, need to form part of the plot line.

So, when it comes to creating a plot or storyline, remember that routine daily life is insufficient for a successful novel; you need to focus on the extra-ordinary, with a sprinkle of day-to-day life to help the story be both captivating and believable.

Why is plot important?

Characterisation is recognised as being difficult to master because of the complexities of individuals, and the need to reflect these complexities successfully on paper, through the establishment of make-believe characters. Plot, however, can be equally as challenging to grasp for a writer. Without a plot, there really is no story. The time spent in creating an exciting plot is well worth the effort, for this will help ensure the success of your novel.

There are so many reasons why establishing a good plot is important:

- Without a plot there is no substance to the story; just a random series of events.
- A plot provides the excitement or anticipation of a story, which is what captivates the reader.
- A plot helps organise what's happening within the novel; the voice, the characters, their emotions, the setting, the pace and the flow of time.

- The plot provides the focus. Novels cannot be about everything, they are focused around a finite number of events and characters. The plot provides this focus, and thus draws everything together into one successful piece of fiction.

Take a minute to think about a fiction book that you've read lately that you really enjoyed; something that captivated you from the very beginning. What was it about the storyline that you loved? How can you learn from this book in order to shape your own enticing plot line or series of plot lines?

The protagonist

Plot lines, well central plot lines anyway (more on subplots later), focus on one leading character. This lead character is known as the protagonist. Ebenbach (*Gotham Writers' Workshop: Writing Fiction, 2008*) describes the protagonist nicely. He states: 'The protagonist is, simply enough, the lead character in your work. He or she will be the most complex and dimensional character in the piece, the one illuminated most fully and followed most closely'.

As the central character in your novel, it is this individual's story, challenge, issue or plight that will dominate your fiction story. So much attention needs to be given to this one character's story that it is very difficult to have more than one protagonist in a novel.

Following the plight or challenge of a protagonist shapes the principle plot line for a reader. Generally plots have a four-part structure:

1. The protagonist wants something – he/she has a goal.

2. The protagonist has personal reasons for setting this goal.

3. There is a conflict or barrier to achieving the goal.

4. The protagonist finds a way (either satisfactorily or unsatisfactorily) to overcome the conflict or barrier that has blocked the attainment of their goal.

As readers, as we work our way through a novel, we find ourselves asking if the protagonist will overcome the conflicts and challenges put in front of them in order to achieve their goal. The answer to our question is then provided at the conclusion of the novel.

'The plot provides the focus.'

The table below identifies a number of classical or popular works of fiction. Against each novel title there is both the name of the protagonist and the primary question that the reader asks themselves as they work their way through the novel. Take a look at the table and consider each book in turn. Can you see how the journey of the protagonist and the way in which the reader strives to answer their own questions about the protagonist's journey provides a captivating plot line for the novel? What can you learn from this that could be applied to your own novel?

Novel	Protagonist	The big question
Pride and Prejudice by Jane Austen	Elizabeth Bennet	Will she end up with Mr Darcy?
For Whom the Bell Tolls by Ernest Hemmingway	Robert Jordan	Will he survive his military mission?
East of Eden by John Steinbeck	Cal Trask	Will he be forgiven for the person he turns out to be?
The Catcher in the Rye by J.D. Salinger	Holden Caulfield	Will Holden find 'home'?
The Hunger Games by Suzanne Collins	Katniss Everdeen	Will Katniss survive the Hunger Games?

The protagonist's goal

The protagonist in a novel is striving for something, and ultimately they are striving for an answer to the 'big' question that the reader is posing as they work their way through the book. In *The Catcher in the Rye* for example, Holden is striving to find a place that he belongs, a place that he can call home. At the opening of the book we learn that he hasn't found this place in the family house, and he also doesn't find it in the psychiatric unit where he resides at the time of narrating his story. As a reader we walk with him as he searches for contentment and a sense of self-awareness and belonging. A reader of *The Catcher in the Rye* will, as they work their way through the book, ask 'Will Holden find peace? Will Holden find a place that he belongs?' Holden too, as the protagonist, will ask this question of himself and of his circumstances. For to feel as though he belongs is, ultimately, his goal.

When writing fiction it is important to have identified, as part of your book planning, what the overarching goal of your protagonist will be. For it is this that will shape the plot of your book; it will be introduced to the reader in your novel's introduction, challenged in the middle section of your novel, and then achieved (or not) in the conclusion to your fictional piece.

Goals come in all shapes and sizes! If you are struggling to identify a goal for your lead character, take a look at the list of goal types below to see if any could meet the needs of your protagonist:

Concrete goals	Abstract goals
A job	Power
A relationship	Self-worth
To survive (life)	Comfort
Money	Love
Death	Self-assurance
Qualification	Belonging
A family	Freedom
An ambition – i.e. to run a marathon	Forgiveness
	Peace
	Self-awareness
	Trust
	Adventure

'When writing fiction it is important to have identified, as part of your book planning, what the overarching goal of your protagonist will be.'

Remember too that concrete goals and abstract goals are often intertwined. It may be that a character is striving for a more abstract goal, such as, say, the feeling of self-worth, but that this is also represented by something more concrete in the novel, such as the protagonist's pursuit of a job or their determination to start a family.

The protagonist's conflict

A novel would be boring if it simply identified the lead character, showed the character to be in pursuit of something and then *bang*, the character achieved his or her goal. To make a plot interesting there has to be a conflict, challenge, or series of challenges that the protagonist needs to overcome in order to achieve their goal.

'To make a plot interesting there has to be a conflict, challenge, or series of challenges that the protagonist needs to overcome in order to achieve their goal.'

Conflicts, challenges and obstacles can be external or internal. When planning the plot that will lead your novel, identify the obstacles that your protagonist needs to overcome in order to achieve their goal. Determine if these obstacles will be external, internal or a mixture of both.

External obstacles include:

- Other people.
- Social structures.
- Nature.
- Acts of God.
- Money.
- Weather.
- Health.
- Work.

Internal obstacles include:

- Fear.
- A lack of self-worth.
- A lack of confidence.

Need2Know

- Emotional fragility.

- Pain.

The resolution of conflict

As your novel comes to a conclusion, the reader needs to see if the obstacles that have been placed in front of the protagonist can ultimately be overcome. Successful novels don't make the battle between protagonist and obstacle an easy one to win; after all, readers like to struggle alongside the protagonist as they strive forward to attain their goal. The genre of your writing and the style in which you have written the novel will, in many ways, dictate if the protagonist is to succeed or not. A more sombre critique of the financial difficulties of the modern Western society may not lead the protagonist to the financial stability he craves, for example. However, an uplifting romantic fiction is more likely to conclude with the girl getting the man of her dreams, no matter how hard he may have been to win over!

Subplots

Novels, in comparison to novellas and short stories, are lengthy books to write! This allows writers to introduce more twists and turns to the plot line, and indeed to add in additional or secondary plot lines that provide new elements of the story to the reader.

Subplots are a great way to enhance a novel. They fulfil a number of functions:

- They allow the reader to learn more about other characters that appear in the book.

- They help keep the story real. There are many aspects to life: family life, working life, academic life, social life, financial organisation and personal time. By ensuring that a number of these aspects of life are explored in your novel, you'll be enabling the reader to get more involved in the life of your principle characters, which will captivate their attention further.

- They break up the tension of a story. Principle plot lines can be emotionally draining to a reader. It is nice to include slightly more light-hearted or comical subplots in a novel to stop a story becoming a little too heavy.

- They can move the novel along. Often subplots can speed up the pace or flow of a novel and this is particularly helpful in the middle of a piece of fiction, when the exploration into the primary plot line can become a little slow-paced or stifled.

- They provide a reason for a mid-story climax or epiphany. The principle plot line in a story will be working towards a climax which will be revealed to the reader in the conclusion of the novel – at this point the reader will know if the protagonist overcame the obstacles to attain his or her goal. However by including subplots in a novel, a number of climaxes can be found throughout the text as each subplot is resolved. This adds another element of enjoyment to the novel for the reader.

When planning or creating subplots it is important to remember that they need to work in a way that complements the principle plotline and thus the novel itself. Remember:

- The subplot should not overshadow the principle plot line. It can serve as a contrast or a parallel but it should not 'steal the limelight' so to speak.

- The subplot should work within the context of the overarching plot.

- The subplot should involve characters that have been previously developed earlier in the novel. Whilst it does not need to involve the protagonist, the characters leading this smaller storyline should already be reasonably well known by the reader.

- The structure of a subplot should follow that of the main plot, i.e. there should be a beginning, middle and an ending – the subplot needs to come to some form of believable conclusion.

Summing Up

- Plots are important to novels, for they provide the series of events that take place throughout the book. A strong plot line is focused, exciting and entertaining; it will reflect parts of 'real life' but will have removed the mundane day-to-day events that add nothing to the flow, context or pace of the story.

- Plots are focused on the protagonist of the novel – the leading character. They generally work to a four-point format; the protagonist desires something/has a goal, the protagonist has reasons for wanting to achieve this goal, obstacles are set in the way of the protagonist achieving this goal, and, finally, the reader learns that the goal has been achieved, could be achieved, or has not been achieved.

- Subplots are a good way to enhance the main plot of a novel. They can add a sense of light relief, can help flesh out secondary characters and can move the flow or pace of a novel.

Chapter Six

Characterisation

Ah, characterisation! This area of fiction writing can be so rewarding to both authors and readers alike. By creating characters you are almost giving literary birth to new individuals, people that you will learn to love and who you will know inside out. And indeed, people that readers of your novel will in turn discover and befriend. Yet creating characters is also an area of fiction writing that many authors dread. If a novel is to be successful the characters need to be 'real', they need to be either loveable or dislikeable, but they need to be believable.

Believable characters

There is a definite art to making a character believable and the key lies in you as an author and your ability to really understand your character's background, personality, appearance and motivation. Successful writers often spend a considerable amount of time building their characters and ensuring that they have a realistic depth to them before they even begin to write. Some steps that can be taken to create such depth could be to develop a family tree, visualise their appearance and mannerisms and develop a history for them that explains how and why they now exist in the state and time that they do within your story.

Having developed all of these factors and created a believable character within your own mind it is then vital that you are able to portray all of this information to the reader. This does not necessarily mean that you have to detail every moment of your character's life from birth until now, instead you should be able to describe your character with conviction and in such a way that the reader can imagine the same history and appearance etc. that you envisaged at the character's 'creative birth'.

'If a novel is to be successful the characters need to be "real", they need to be either loveable or dislikeable, but they need to be believable.'

Descriptive passages are essential to help readers associate with a character, even the simplest definition of how a character walks or nervously plays with their hair, for example, can say so much about the character and will quickly help the reader to get to know them and believe in them. Speech is another important factor in making a character believable, and as you write, you should be able to hear the character in your head and in doing so you should be able to portray the precise way in which they would speak, again adding to the believability.

In essence, the key to building a believable character is to ensure that you build them with depth and that you write in such a way that allows the reader to understand that depth.

Some key things to remember when creating believable characters are:

- Ensure your character has a purpose for existing within the story.

- Know your character's motivation.

- Know your character's background.

- Know your character's appearance, mannerisms and voice.

- Use narrative and descriptive passages to portray all of the above elements.

We'll look at each of these areas throughout this chapter and chapter 7.

'If a character is truly driven and motivated to achieve something, then this motivation is hugely exciting for a fiction reader.'

Motivation and desire

We saw in chapter 5 that the main plot of a novel will focus on a protagonist – a lead character – and will follow the story of the character as he or she seeks to attain a goal; something they need, want or desire. By default then, a character must have a desire, and they must be motivated to try and obtain the thing that they desire, whether it be a tangible or abstract goal. The character's motivating desire can be to achieve or obtain something big and life-changing, or small and moment-changing. In this instance size doesn't matter, what matters is the strength of the desire. If a character is truly driven and motivated to achieve something, then this motivation is hugely exciting for a fiction reader.

The desire a character holds, and their motivation to fulfil this desire, moves a story forward. It provides pace, it provides energy, and it helps bring a character to life. Lovely!

As you start to build up a profile for the protagonist that will lead your novel, think about what it is that they are striving for in your story. Ask yourself the following questions:

- What is the significant event that dominates the plot line? What is it that your protagonist wants? What's their goal?

- What does the protagonist hope to achieve by reaching this goal? What is it that they really desire?

- Why do they have this goal?

- What is the driving force behind them continuously and relentlessly striving forward to achieve their goal?

- Aside from this particular journey, where the character is working to achieve a particular goal or desire, what generally motivates your character? And why?

By responding to these questions you'll be able to learn a little more about your own protagonist's desires and motivations. Once you have this awareness, you'll find it easier to convey to your readers through your novel writing.

Creating 'real' characters

As stated earlier in this chapter, it is one thing to create a character for your novel, quite another to create a believable character. Yet for a novel to really work, all characters need to be believable to the very varied and diverse readership your book will attract. Part of the method for creating these very real characters is in recognising that characters, like people, are very complex. We don't all fall into a type – in fact in our totality none of us fall into a type as we are all in fact unique. Recognise the many sides to a person as you draw up a character and respect this level of individuality as far as possible. Remember, there is more to stock brokers than significant wealth and long working hours. There is more to stay-at-home mums than housework, creative child play and coffee shops, and there is more to teenagers than just a desire to rebel.

Creating characters that are believable, that are 'real', thus represents one of the great challenges that fiction writers encounter. Here we shall investigate some of the more difficult 'human' qualities that writers struggle to embed within their own personally created characters. These qualities are:

- The way in which humans display contrasting traits.

- The fact that personalities are generally consistent throughout life.

- The added complication of the fact that people can, at times, change.

Contrasting traits

Reissenweber *(Gotham Writers' Workshop: Writing Fiction, 2008)* reminds us of one of the complexities of human beings: 'A fascinating element of human nature is that we all possess contrasting traits, sometimes subtle, other times greatly conflicting. These contrasts provide endless opportunity to make your characters complex'.

'When creating lead characters for your novel, think about the way in which they can display contrasting characteristics.'

When creating lead characters for your novel, think about the way in which they can display contrasting characteristics. Remember that the characteristics should always remain within the realms of believability for your character – they should not stick out like a sore thumb. Some examples of contrasting characteristics (from *safaribooksonline.com*) are provided below as thinking points for you:

- They are tough and mean, but terrified of snakes, spiders or rats.

- They are brutal and evil, but have a soft spot for women and won't allow them to be harmed.

- They are meek and mild ordinarily, but will fight like a tiger when cornered.

- They are a magnificent performer, but shy and awkward when not performing.

- They are powerful and successful, but in private they are a mass of worries, anxieties and low self-esteem.

- They are awkward and socially inept, but have an intellect the size of the Pacific Ocean.

- They seem to have no emotional response to life, except when they are alone and they weep copiously.

Consistent personalities

Yes, characters need to display contrasting traits at times in order for them to take on a persona that readers can relate to. However, as stated previously, these traits need to remain within the boundaries of the character's overarching personality. Individuals do not display wild changes in their personalities and therefore neither should your characters.

Remember, contrasting traits and the ability to change one particular part of a personality are all very normal elements of a human being. Swinging from one personality type to another on a random or ad hoc basis is not, however, typical behaviour and therefore characters that change their personality dramatically throughout a novel will render themselves unbelievable to the reader.

People can change

This may all sound very contradictory, hence the difficulty of successfully displaying these complexities of humans in literary characters, but people can, at times, change. And where it is appropriate, as a writer, you should reflect this ability to change in the characters that you create.

Writers will often use a character's ability to change as part of the climax, epiphany or conclusion to a novel. A character may strive forward to reach their goal, let's say that they are searching for their long-lost father, and this task may be full of obstacles that ultimately they don't overcome. However, by the end of the book we may see this motivating desire dull in the character, as they come to the realisation that they were looking for their father in order to try to gain a higher level of self-awareness. What they recognise, however, is that self-awareness comes from within, and so their determination to meet the father who does not want to be found changes.

Getting to know your characters

Characters are individuals who you create when you commit their stories to paper. In order to portray your characters well on paper, however, you need to know them inside out first. This involves a lot of planning and character sketching, and whilst this may take time, it will pay dividends in the long run as you'll find that the way that you convey the characters in your novel is smooth, fluid and believable.

The table below outlines four important categories to consider when scoping out your lead characters. Against each category there are a series of questions that will help you shape a well-rounded and very 'real' character to lead your novel.

Remember, that whilst you won't use all of the information about your characters that you glean from this exercise, it will nonetheless help you identify with your character and thus create a solid identity for them within your novel. As E.M. Forster wrote in Aspects of the Novel, a character is real when the author knows everything there is to know about him or her: 'He may not choose to tell all he knows – many of the facts, even the kind we call obvious, may be hidden. But he will give us the feeling that though the character has not been explained, it is explicable . . .'

Characteristic category	Questions to consider
Appearance	What colour hair does your character have?
	What colour eyes does your character have?
	What distinguishes your character (physically) from others?

Characteristic category	Questions to consider
Background	Where and when was your character born? Where has he or she lived subsequently? Has your character been in love before? What happened? Which childhood memories are the strongest?
Personality	Is your character close to his or her family members? Who does he or she socialise with? How does your character react when he or she is angry? What is his or her biggest fear? Why? What makes your character laugh?
Primary identity	What is the name of your character? Are they called this routinely? What does your character eat? What does he or she like and dislike? How does your character sit? How does your character dress? How does your character spend a weekend? Map out a typical Sunday for him or her.

Show, tell and action!

That wonderful phrase 'show, don't tell' haunts writers as they work to commit their characters to paper. All writers know the importance of showing the reader that a character possesses a particular quality or completes a particular action as opposed to just stating that they do so. We don't tell the audience that our protagonist is shy for example, we show them actions that demonstrate the shyness of the character. All very well and good to know this important piece of creative writing theory, but how do you achieve this in reality?

Below are 5 top tips on how to let your characters display their own personalities through the power of action as opposed to narration:

1. Use detail. Description is a great way to force you to show the reader what's happening and how something appears.

2. Cover all five senses as you describe the actions of your characters. How does something smell to them? What can they see? What do the objects around them feel like etc.?

3. Have other characters talk about your protagonist and his or her actions.

4. Utilise dialogue to display how a character behaves, thinks or acts. (See chapter 7 for more information on creating well-crafted dialogue).

5. Don't be afraid to tell sometimes. Yes it is better to show the reader how a character thinks, feels and acts. But this can't be done *all* the time. Sometimes you need to just state an action or a thought and then move the story on. 'He cried' for example, or 'he'd never liked spiders'.

'When a reader "hears" the name of a character for the first time, they will automatically conjure up an image of that character in their head, and these first conceptions are hard to change.'

That all-important name

Character names are important. When a reader 'hears' the name of a character for the first time, they will automatically conjure up an image of that character in their head, and these first conceptions are hard to change. It is therefore best to ensure that the name of a character fits their personality, their circumstances and their lifestyle. The name Hortense brings to mind a character that is very different from, say, Mary.

Coming up with a name that fits your character can feel like a difficult process. First, brainstorm all of the possible names that your character could hold. Look in phone books, in baby naming books, and even utilise online name-generating software systems to come up with a list of contenders. Then apply some simple rules:

- Don't use a name that belongs to someone famous.

- Be happy that the name reflects the personality of your character.

- Be sure that the name chosen fits the time period in which your book is set.

- Avoid using names that sound similar in a novel. You don't want your core characters to be named Mike, Mark, Mick and Michelle, for example.

- Avoid trendy names to ensure that your characters are relevant for decades to come.

Summing Up

- The most important task a writer has when focusing on characterisation is to keep their characters believable and 'real'.

- Identify what motivates a character.

- Ensure that they display behaviour that reflects human nature; i.e. their personalities are consistent and they can, at times, change their behaviours for the better.

- Learn all about a character by mapping their appearances, their backgrounds, their personal identity and their personality.

- Use the text to show the reader how a character thinks, feels and behaves.

- Provide the character with a name that fits their personality and circumstance.

Need2Know

Chapter Seven

Dialogue

Ah dialogue – the tool that the majority of us use each day to convey what we think, believe, want, wish for, hope, feel and know. Dialogue is the conversational exchange between two or more individuals. Dialogue can therefore take on a written form, i.e. through the use of a series of emails, letters or text messages between individuals. Primarily, however, dialogue is spoken.

In reality of course, normally dialogue comes easily to us all. We chat away happily to friends and family members without consciously thinking about what we're about to say next and how to phrase what it is that we want to say. I say 'normally' here because I am sure that we've all been in situations with other individuals where dialogue is necessary, but where it is forced or difficult. Consider for example, a student's first day on campus, or a blind date, or a relationship break-up. These situations often bring with them the need for dialogue, but this dialogue is difficult or forced.

Authors often find dialogue difficult to convey in fiction novels. It can feel forced, irrelevant, or not in-keeping with the physical description of the character that has previously been displayed in the writing. Dialogue is, however, an important part of novel writing. Remember that in chapter 6 we outlined the importance of showing the reader, not telling the reader? Well what better way of showing the reader what's happening through dialogue? It's so much better than summarising an event!

How to make dialogue sound real

One of the reasons that writers dread creating dialogue for their characters is that they fear that the dialogue will not sound real; that it will be stilted and will scream out that the world they've worked so hard to create is indeed simply a novel, and not something that the reader can become a part of or connect with. One of the success criterion for a novel therefore, is to ensure that the dialogue used sounds real; that it 'works' for the novel.

Characters will ultimately sound real and thus more natural when they use dialogue that suits them and the context within which they exist. The words that characters mutter should match their personality, their situation, cultural background and time period. In a nutshell, dialogue should be written to mimic the way that people actually talk.

For example, if you have a character in your novel who is English, using particularly English expressions in his or her speech is a great way to indicate the character's heritage, home country and background. Similarly, a Victorian character would speak decidedly differently from a more contemporary character. And if you are writing a young adult fiction, no doubt the protagonist will be a teenager, and will therefore need to speak in a way that reflects contemporary teenage expressions and lingo.

Remember too that nowadays, when we're conversing, we generally tend to speak in incomplete sentences, use contractions, and fall prey to imperfect grammar. Contemporary characters within a novel will therefore need to follow these speech patterns if they are to remain believable to the reader. Character dialogue that is grammatically perfect and sentences that are perfectly constructed will thus sound less natural.

'Characters will ultimately sound real and thus more natural when they use dialogue that suits them and the context within which they exist.'

Character interaction

The interaction we see in novels that takes place between characters is so much more than just the spoken word; yet dialogue is at the centre of conversation. Consider the different characters that are generally mixed up together in a story. Some characters are related, some are good friends, some are good enemies, some are purely acquaintances – the relationship ties we witness in a novel mirror those seen in real life. Therefore different kinds of characters in a story will naturally interact in different ways.

For dialogue to sound real, character interaction should suit the characters involved. Two sisters, for example, will naturally interact with each other differently from two indifferent acquaintances. The language used in a conversation between the two sisters would therefore likely be more familiar and informal than the dialogue seen between the acquaintances.

Dialogue tags

Dialogue tags are the little phrases that an author adds to the beginning or end of a dialogue entry to help indicate who has said something, and how it has been said.

Dialogue tags can both add to and hinder a series of dialogue. An excess of 'he said' or 'she said' for example, can stifle the flow of the conversation between the characters. When creating dialogue tags try instead to find the most accurate word to describe the dialogue. Here again we see the importance of expanding your knowledge of vocabulary!

As a helpful exercise, try to come up with 20 alternative dialogue tags to 'she said', that better reflect a character's tone and meaning in differing circumstances.

In addition, consider alternatives to dialogue tags that can also help describe a character's mood and tone of voice. Body language, for example, is about as important as words in a conversation. A character's body language, if properly described, indicates the character's mood, sets the tone for the conversation, and gives the reader a better idea of what the dialogue itself sounds like. Smiling, arm waving, eye rolling, shrugging and sighing are all great examples of indicative body language.

The following two exercises can help with writing natural sounding dialogue:

1. People watching – Observing others as they interact, as they speak with each other and drawing on life's real conversations.

2. Reading dialogue out loud – acting out the dialogue, including body language and facial expressions helps to know whether the dialogue sounds natural, and also helps determine accurate dialogue tags.

'For dialogue to sound real, character interaction should suit the characters involved.'

Indirect dialogue

Generally, when referring to dialogue, it is active dialogue that is meant; where the actual lines that are spoken are written down in the text, using speech marks and dialogue tags to support the reader's understanding of the conversation as a whole.

However, there are times when indirect dialogue can be quite handy! Imagine, for example, that you want to convey the contents of a conversation to the reader, but you don't want this to slow the pace of the storyline at that particular moment in time. This is the time to use indirect dialogue. Within indirect dialogue, the contents of a conversation can be conveyed to the reader as a summary.

The best way to illustrate the benefits of writing in this way is to look at an example. Below is a passage from Tobias Wolff's book *Smokers*. In this particular passage, the narrator is accosted by an annoying boy who is travelling to the same boarding school as the narrator:

'He started to talk almost the moment he sat down, and he didn't stop until we reached Wallingford. Was I going to Choate? What a coincidence – so was he. My first year? His too. Where was I from? Oregon?'

By using indirect speech in this way the reader is able to understand a little more about both the annoying boy and the narrator, but the pace is not slowed by the need to recite the full conversation in active dialogue.

'A character's body language, if properly described, indicates the character's mood, sets the tone for the conversation, and gives the reader a better idea of what the dialogue itself sounds like.'

Bad dialogue

Dialogue can go wrong – no doubt about it. And as explained at the beginning of the chapter, poor dialogue can discredit a lot of the positive characterisation, plot line and description that has been lovingly crafted. It is therefore important to spend time reviewing the dialogue that your characters speak, to ensure that it is as authentic and appropriate as possible. A number of key pitfalls to avoid are outlined here:

- Dialogue is generally not the best way to expose facts about characters or circumstances. If you are going to expose facts to the reader through dialogue, do it in a way that the reader can see a credible reason for introducing this information to them through speech at the given point in time.

- Don't use your characters as a mechanism for preaching to the reader.

- Keep the dialogue in line with the character's age, personality, social setting and period of existence.

- Read and then re-read the dialogue between characters to ensure that there aren't any instances of their conversations sounding forced or unrealistic.

Incorporating dialect

Dialect can be a nightmare in novels. It is hard to reflect a character's dialect well, and when dialect isn't written well it becomes very distracting for the reader.

If you do want to incorporate dialect into a novel, remember:

- Focus on simply giving a flavour of dialect to the reader; no more and no less.

- Look to include key or defining words that portray a particular dialect, rather than writing all of a character's dialogue in dialect-driven language.

- Provide the speech patterns and rhythms of a dialect to convey authenticity.

- Allow a character to comment on the accent or dialect of another character as this will quickly and succinctly explain to the reader that the character has a particular speech pattern.

'Poor dialogue can discredit a lot of the positive characterisation, plot line and description that has been lovingly crafted.'

Summing Up

■ Writers are often fearful of creating dialogue for characters, as it can be difficult to create dialogue that is in-keeping with the personality of the character that is speaking.

■ Reflect the personality, social stance, time period and age of the character.

■ Individuals do not normally speak perfectly; we all mess about with grammar, tenses, sentence construction and meaning as we talk – the same should be true of characters in novels.

■ Indirect dialogue can be a useful way of summarising a conversation without slowing the flow of the storyline.

■ Dialect should always be handled with care!

Need2Know

Chapter Eight

Narration

Having now looked at the way in which dialogue works in a novel, and how it can both bring a story to life and move the plot line forward, it can be difficult to see what role narration plays within a novel; after all the novel clearly has a leading voice that is 'telling' their story.

Narration, however, is important because it offers some structure and balance to the novel. Dialogue is there to convey the thoughts and words of characters, narration is there to fill in the blanks – to provide context, setting, pace and flow to the plot. As Wikipedia nicely summarises for us: 'A narrative is a constructive format (as a work of speech, writing, song, film, television, video games, photography or theatre) that describes a sequence of non-fictional or fictional events'.

'Dialogue is there to convey the thoughts and words of characters, narration is there to fill in the blanks – to provide context, setting, pace and flow to the plot.'

Narrative styles

There are a number of different narrative styles that a writer can utilise when creating a novel. Let's explore each one in turn; first person, first person peripheral, third person, third person omniscient, and second person.

First person narrative

This is where the story is narrated by the protagonist. As it is a character who is dictating the novel, the novel is written using the word 'I'. 'I saw him shoot her', 'I tasted the cherry pie', 'I wished we'd stayed longer', 'I hate her sometimes', and so on.

Taken from Margaret Atwood's story *Weight*, the following paragraph illustrates the use of the first person narrative:

'I am gaining weight. I'm not getting bigger, only heavier. This doesn't show up on the scales: technically, I'm the same. My clothes still fit, so it isn't size, what they tell you about fat taking up more space than muscle. The heaviness I feel is in the energy I burn up getting myself around: along the sidewalk, up the stairs, through the day. It's the pressure on my feet. It's a density of the cells, as if I've been drinking heavy metals'.

First person peripheral

This is where the story is narrated by a secondary character, i.e. not the protagonist. Again, the use of 'I' is used throughout the novel.

F.S. Fitzgerald uses the first person peripheral narration style in *The Great Gatsby*. In the following paragraph we see Nick Carraway, the narrator, observe and relate to the principle plot line from afar:

'And as I sat there, brooding on the old unknown world, I thought of Gatsby's wonder when he first picked out the green light at the end of Daisy's dock. He had come a long way to this blue lawn and his dreams must have seemed so close that he could hardly fail to grasp it'.

Third person

Told in third person means the story is narrated by a person who is not involved in the novel at all – this person may, for example, be the author. As it isn't a character that is dictating the story, the pronouns 'he', 'she' and 'they' are used – 'he liked her', 'he wasn't sure how to act', 'she had enjoyed their sandwich together', 'they walked gracefully through the park'.

In *Lucky Jim* by Kingsley Amis, we see how the use of third person narration can convey the narrator's views of others and their situations, which often differs from how the individuals view their own lives or characters. For example:

'[Dixon] tried to flair his features into some sort of response to humour. Mentally, however, he was making a different face and promising himself he'd made it actually when next alone. He'd drawn his lower lip in under his top lip and by

> 'Told in third person means the story is narrated by a person who is not involved in the novel at all – this person may, for example, be the author.'

degrees retract his chin as far as possible, all this while dilating his eyes and nostrils. By these means he would, he was confident, cause a deep and dangerous flush to suffuse his face'.

Third person omniscient

This is where the narrator is almost God-like in the way they dictate the story. They see everything and hold no bias towards the way in which the action is unfolding, and they switch their narration to reflect the thoughts and actions of different characters within the novel. Again, the pronouns 'he', 'she' and 'they' are all used to narrate the story.

Omniscient narratives are less common for novels written in the twentieth century. Below is a passage from one of the rare twentieth century novels that uses the third person omniscient point of view, Eudora Welty's *No Place for You, My Love*:

'It must stick out all over me, she thought, so people think they can love me or hate me just by looking at me. How did it leave us – the old, safe, slow way people used to know of learning how another feels, and the privilege that went with it of shying away if it seemed best? People in love like me, I suppose, give away the short cuts to everybody's secrets'.

'Omniscient narratives are less common for novels written in the twentieth century.'

Second person

Second person narration is where the narrator talks directly to the reader and puts forward their thoughts and opinions by using the pronoun 'you'. 'You didn't like their attitude', 'you found their relationship frustrating', 'you'd missed something – of this you were sure'.

Whilst difficult to keep the second person narration interesting for an entire book, Helen Dunmore successfully does so in her novel *With Your Crooked Heart*:

'You lie down on the warm stone, and wriggle your body until it fits. Then you relax, and the terrace bears you up as if you are floating out to sea. Sun has been pouring onto it since seven o'clock, and every grain of stone is packed

with heat. Sun pours on to the glistening mound of your belly, onto your parted thighs, your arms, your fingers, your face. No part of you resists, no part does not shine'.

Which style suits your writing?

Deciding upon a narrative style to use within your book will either be deliberate or will be pre-determined by the manner in which you write. There are pros and cons to all of the narrative styles listed, and these are explored in the following table. However when it comes to choosing how to narrate your story, the most important thing to remember is that you must be comfortable with writing in that particular narration style. Choose a narration style that you find easy to follow through, for it is such an integral part of the novel, and your writing experiences will be so much harder than they need to be if you try to narrate the story through a voice that you really can't identify with.

'Your writing experiences will be so much harder than they need to be if you try to narrate the story through a voice that you really can't identify with.'

The following table below outlines some of the primary benefits and weaknesses of each narrative style. Consider each in turn before deciding the manner through which you will narrate your novel.

Narration style	Pros	Cons
First person	The reader has an immediate connection with the protagonist which allows a sense of intimacy. It is generally easier to write in the first person. It is easy to adopt an open, chatty and approachable tone, which can engage readers.	The story is dominated by one lead character, in both plot line and now language. Talking about 'I, I, I' all the time can make a novel feel a little claustrophobic. It can be much harder to show rather than tell when using the first person, as the narrative tends to get blocked with the lead character telling the reader what he or she thinks, did or feels. Description is often lost. Unless the character has a particular pull towards a setting or location, the reader doesn't learn about it. The author is forced to always use the one voice when explaining an event. Subplots need to in some way involve the protagonist, so that he or she can comment on them.

Narration style	Pros	Cons
First person peripheral	As before, however the intimacy that is built up is in relation to the narrator of the book, a secondary character, as opposed to the protagonist.	As before, however with this form of narration the reader is able to learn in detail about both the protagonist and the narrator. Furthermore, subplots will need to involve the narrator only (through an observatory role) and not necessarily the protagonist.
Third person	It allows the author to write paragraphs or chapters from the point of view of different characters. More than one character can be developed in full. The author can achieve a strong balance between action, character description and a focus on the thoughts and opinions of the lead characters. Subplots containing any character can easily be conveyed.	The reader loses the deep connection with the protagonist – they can't get as close to the lead character as they would in a novel written in first person narration. It can be difficult to correctly balance the time spent on hearing the protagonist's voice, hearing the voices and thoughts of secondary characters and on conveying action and description.

Need2Know

Narration style	Pros	Cons
Third person omniscient	It is a traditional way to narrate a story. The reader is able to get to know a number of characters in great detail, for the insight they receive into each character is generally of the same quantity. You have freedom over the language and tone used – even when speaking about a 5-year-old child, the language used can reflect that of the narrator – not be limited to the words of the child. The narrator can discuss a number of threads of the story and the subplots with ease – they are not limited to those storylines that directly affect them. Action and description can be focused upon, as opposed to being led by the feelings, thoughts and speech of an individual character.	An omniscient narration often exposes the author – and so the reader is aware of the presence of the writer when reading the novel. It can be difficult for the reader to feel a sense of intimacy with the characters, which in turn can make it difficult for them to care about the characters' stories.

Narration style	Pros	Cons
Second person	The reader can feel as if he or she is the protagonist, and thus is drawn directly into the action of the novel. The author's voice is not heard; the book focuses on the reader's reaction to the story, not the author's thoughts about the story.	It is generally a disliked form of narration. It is difficult to convey thoughts and feelings, as the author does not know how the reader (the 'you') will respond to particular events or actions.

'Often a multiple narrator style is chosen for novels that tell the reader of one particular event or plot line, but from the point of view of two or more characters that were involved in this event or series of actions.'

Multiple narrators

Whilst the majority of novels are written from the point of view of just one individual; be that in the first, second or third narrative style, some authors do choose to use a multiple point of view or vision when creating their novel. This can be achieved using the first or third person narrative style. Often a multiple narrator style is chosen for novels that tell the reader of one particular event or plot line, but from the point of view of two or more characters that were involved in this event or series of actions. In *The Sweet Hereafter* by Russell Banks, for example, four first person narrators are used to tell and then retell the story of a tragic school bus crash. In this story the reader 'sees' the crash from the point of view of the bus driver; a man whose two small children were killed in the crash; a New York City negligence attorney and a teenage girl injured in the accident.

When writing a novel that uses multiple narrators, remember:

- Keep the narration provided by each narrating character balanced. Give equal 'airtime' to each of the characters in order to allow the reader to engage with each, and to provide a sense of balance to the novel as a whole.

- Avoid confusion! Make sure it is clear which character is narrating at any given time.

- Break the story up logically. Ensure that the switches in narrator make sense to the flow of the novel in its entirety.

Summing Up

▨ It is important for the flow, style and structure of a novel that you as the author determine who will be narrating the story. As we have seen, this can either be a character, a number of characters, the reader, or you – the author.

▨ There are pros and cons to each narrative style, and each should be considered in detail before embarking on a novel. Regardless of which narrating style you choose, be sure to keep the style consistent throughout the book.

▨ Multiple narrators can at times enhance a story; particularly if you want to focus on the reactions of a number of characters to one particular event. Be sure, however, to keep a balance between each of the narrators, so that the reader can establish a solid relationship with each of them.

Chapter Nine

Description

What is description?

In this chapter we explore the notion of description. So, firstly let's focus on a definition of description. Within the contents of fiction writing, what exactly is 'description'?

The Business Dictionary defines the term description as: 'A detailed account of the certain or salient aspects, characteristics or features of a subject matter or something seen, heard, or otherwise experienced or known'.

This definition identifies the fact that to describe is to outline, in detail, the elements or aspects of something or someone. *Webster's New World Dictionary* adds a little creative element to the definition of the verb 'describe'. It offers two helpful definitions:

1. 'To tell or write about; give a detailed account of'.

2. 'To picture in words'.

Whilst the first definition mirrors that seen in *The Business Dictionary,* the second is much more poetic – to describe is to create a picture in the reader's mind. When description is effective it is the writing tool that pulls the reader into the world that exists within the novel. It is powerful description that forces the reader out of their armchair, out of their hectic family life, out of their difficult relationship and into the coffee shop where the characters sit. Poor description, however, leaves the reader recognising that the world about which they're reading is only a story, and one which they cannot identify with, believe in or become a part of. When a reader engrosses themselves within a book that is weak in terms of description, they are fully aware of their hectic family life, of their arguments with their partner, of their work frustrations; they are unable to become fully involved in the story that lies in front of them for they

'When description is effective it is the writing tool that pulls the reader into the world that exists within the novel. When description is bad, a reader recognises a novel for what it is; a story. Nothing more.'

cannot put belief or faith into this story or the plot that is being played out before them. When description is bad, a reader recognises a novel for what it is; a story. Nothing more.

Using all of the five senses

It sounds a little mad but if you are a writer, you need to take notice of all of your senses, all of the time! This statement is particularly important to novel writers, who, as we've discussed already, rely on strong description to bring their story to life when captured in writing.

A well-written piece will pull on all of the reader's senses to really draw them into the writing. Finding a way to ensure that all of your reader's senses are sufficiently tantalised, however, can be more challenging than you may initially think. So one of the best ways to easily weave information that appeals to all senses into your writing is to spend time each day taking notice of your own senses, and how they are stimulated by day-to-day activities and surroundings.

Below are some day-to-day experiences that can appeal to a range of our senses. Think about how your own senses react when they come into contact with each of the following:

- Newly washed laundry – smell, touch.
- A newborn baby – smell, touch, sight, sound.
- A traffic jam – sight, sound, smell.
- Animals – all senses.
- Your lover – sight, touch, smell.
- Freshly cut lawn – smell, touch and sight.
- Freshly brewed coffee – smell.

Each of these experiences appeal to a number of our senses, and yet when they are used in writing, they are often only portrayed in a way that appeals to one of the reader's senses. We might learn about what a character's lover looks like, but we don't necessarily know what impact the visual sighting of the character's lover has on the character, or how their lover smells or what they feel like to touch. By adding in these additional dimensions, a writer would find that their readers connect much more with the characters contained within their stories. Incidentally, the same is true with non-fiction writing. Even if an article or book is based around factual information, it still needs to appeal to and engage the reader; and the best way to do this is to ensure that the writer has used language within their writing that is based around all five of the senses; touch, sight, sound, taste and smell.

The following passage of text is from Amy Tan's novel *Rules of the Game*. It is a brilliant piece of fiction writing which nicely utilises all five of the senses when describing a home:

'We lived on Waverly Place, in a warm, clean, two-bedroom flat that sat above a small Chinese bakery, specialising in steamed pastries and dim sum. In the early morning, when the alley was still quiet, I could smell fragrant red beans as they were cooked down to a pasty sweetness. By daybreak, our flat was heavy with the odour of fried sesame balls and sweet curried chicken crescents. From my bed, I would listen as my father got ready for work, then locked the door behind him, one-two-three clicks'.

So, as you start to look at the way in which you use description within your novel, be sure to check that the draft chapters that you're creating utilise language that appeals to all five senses. Think about each of the individual settings or situations that you have described or included within your writing. Can they be portrayed in a different way in order to ensure that they appeal to a range of senses?

Describing a character

When we think of description, we often think of the language used to portray a place, an event or a bond. The creation of a character, however, is also hugely dependent upon the use of descriptive language, as we've explored in chapter 6.

In order to engage with the characters in a book, the reader must have some sense of how the characters look. A character's appearance not only helps the reader to visualise them, but it also tells us a lot about the character's personality and, at times, about their emotions and circumstances.

It might be tempting to think that the best way forward is to sketch out in words how the character looks all in one hit – one large paragraph or series of paragraphs that visually describes the person the reader is about to learn more about. However this is quite a stilted approach to writing and can leave the book, or that particular section of the book, relatively flat. Instead, a writer needs to weave in information about a character's appearance in an almost subconscious manner, so that the reader finds that they are learning a lot about the character, without having to wade through large chunks of descriptive text.

Within fiction writing there are 5 key ways of showing appearance:

1. Static description.

2. Dialogue.

3. Emotional reaction.

4. Thoughts.

5. Actions.

Static description is useful if you want to convey a quick piece of visual information about a character in a short sentence – 'his hair was grey' – etc. However, this form of description is usually quite disinteresting and flat. It also doesn't allow the reader to learn anything more about the character; yes we may know that he or she has grey hair, but we don't know anything further about their personality. Readers of fiction need to feel something towards the characters they are reading about, so in all characterisation there is a need to add some emotion to give the writing life and vitality.

As we saw in chapter 6, names can be a useful way to add life to a character through the power of description. A middle-aged female would not, for example, conjure up the same image in the reader's mind if they were called Lara as they would if they were called Wendy. The name Lara suggests someone who is younger, perhaps thinner and certainly an individual who is contemporary. In comparison, a character with the name Wendy does fit with her middle-aged description, and the reader would assume that she is a more reserved and traditional character than Lara would appear to be. It is therefore

'A writer needs to weave in information about a character's appearance in an almost subconscious manner, so that the reader finds that they are learning a lot about the character, without having to wade through large chunks of descriptive text.'

important to ensure that the names you give your characters fit with the way in which you will want to describe them, for even just through hearing a character's name the reader will begin to form visual images of him or her.

When adding in character description, remember too to think about all of the senses. The perfume that an individual wears will tell the reader a lot about them, the way their skin feels will help the reader draw parallels with the character's personality, as will any distinctive accents or particular patterns of speech. Clothes are also an important element of characterisation as they tell us so much about what the character likes to wear, how they feel about their body, their social status and their personal self-esteem.

The importance of language

It is language that we use to create novels, and when it comes to description in storytelling, the language used needs to be specific, accurate and relevantly detailed. Let's review each of these essential elements in turn.

Be specific!

It is not enough to use all five of the senses to describe a scene. You need descriptions to be specific and personal if they are going to really convey meaning and draw the reader into the novel. When talking about the importance of being specific in description, Lobardi (*Gotham Writers' Workshop: Writing Fiction, 2008*) pulls on the example of the following description: 'his intense grey eyes'. He recalls a story where, when presented with this line of description, a friend of his asked, 'What is really meant here?'

And what was meant? Well the author had meant to convey that the eyes of the character were slate-grey, and that they glittered a little, as if he had extra tear ducts. This level of specific detail is not, however, conveyed in the simple line: 'His intense grey eyes'.

When it comes to description it is so easy to rush in with vague adjectives with the expectation that these will quickly build up a picture for the reader. But specific descriptions are needed if the reader is to be fully pulled into the novel.

'When adding in character description, remember too to think about all of the senses.'

This element of novel writing is a skill that can take time to master. When describing scenes or characters keep asking yourself, what do I mean here? Does the descriptive writing used conjure up the full picture that I can see in my creative mind? If not, how can this be enhanced? It can also be useful to practise describing with specifics. Think of a person who is close to you, for example. Then, on paper, describe them specifically. Try to capture their uniqueness through the written word.

Be accurate

Accuracy within novel writing comes from always using exactly the right word to describe something or someone. As Mark Twain famously noted, the difference between using the right word and the almost right word is the difference between lightning and a lightning bug. Often the right words flow from your fingers as you write. But on occasion, as a writer, you may find that you cannot quite portray the picture you can visualise. When examples of this appear in your text, be sure to review them and reflect upon the accuracy of your language; is each word perfect?

'Use adverbs and adjectives to support description – but don't use them as your only means of description.'

Remember the following key tips when searching for accurate descriptions within your novel:

- It is OK to spend half a day identifying the right word! If you feel that a word or a sentence construction isn't quite right, chances are that your reader will stumble over the same word or phrase. Take the time to mend or improve the stumbling block – it will pay dividends in the long run.

- Work to expand your vocabulary. Sometimes an author cannot conjure up the best word to use to describe a person, event, place or experience simply because they aren't aware of the most fitting word. By enhancing your vocabulary you'll be minimising the possibility of this difficulty happening to you.

- Use adverbs and adjectives to support description – but don't use them as your only means of description. A sentence that is full of adjectives not only screams 'lazy writer', but it is also often difficult to unpick when searching for the meaning of the sentence. Instead, think about how unusual verbs can convey powerful description, i.e. 'she glided', or 'she floated'.

Keep it relevant

As authors, we must be cautious however; as with all good things in life, less is generally more. It can be tempting to run away with description in a novel; to throw in all five senses at each descriptive opportunity, to focus on fancy terminology, verbs, adverbs and adjectives to push a piece of fiction writing forward. Try to resist the temptation at times! You need to ensure that your descriptive details have been well chosen and conveyed to the reader for a purpose. There is nothing more off-putting than trawling through a novel that is laden down with thick description. The plot is lost and ultimately so is the reader. Novel writing is about balancing the elements of fiction writing in a way that keeps the book enticing for the reader. Description, just like plot lines and dialogue, needs to remain well balanced too.

Clichés

Clichés should be avoided at all costs. A cliché is a trite or overused expression or idea. And as it is overused, it therefore becomes meaningless when said, expressed or written. Clichés can signify poor descriptive ability within a novel. A few common clichés to avoid in your novel writing include:

- Bone-chilling cold.
- Her cascading hair.
- Sleeping like the dead.
- Turning on one's heel.
- Feet planted firmly on the floor.

'Clichés can signify poor descriptive ability within a novel.'

Summing Up

- Description is the writing tool authors use to help paint a picture of what's happening within the novel.

- Description should involve all five of the senses for it to successfully portray a scene, item, person or event.

- When writing descriptive language it is important to remain focused. Descriptions should be detailed, accurate and meaningful.

- Finally, remember that when it comes to description less is often more!

- Avoid using clichés, their use can indicate a poor descriptive ability as an author.

Chapter Ten

The Writing Process

Committing your ideas to paper

So, now that you've worked through the theory of how to create a novel, and you've finalised the planning, research and preparation stage of your work, the next step is to commit your story to paper.

As we've discussed before, writing a novel is something that many people aspire to do. Actually writing a novel (and particularly finishing a novel) is a big task and a great achievement. So how do you move from aspiring to write a book, to actually commencing work on a successful and inspired book? This is the question!

Many writers start novels but never finish them. If you want to start a novel *properly* then you need to plan to finish it before even starting it. This means ensuring that you have scheduled sufficient writing time into your daily or weekly timetable to enable the book to not only be started . . . but finished too. This is where your writing timetable is important (see chapter 2). Stick to your timetable as much as possible, even if to do so means that you need to review and revise the way in which you initially allocated writing time when you drew the timetable up.

In addition, be sure that you've completed sufficient research and planning for you to feel confident that you can start writing a well-structured and thought out novel. The level of planning that needs to have taken place for this confidence to be assumed will differ from writer to writer, only you'll know when you're happy with the preparation you've completed.

So, characters, plot line and environment are all determined through the research and planning you've undertaken. What's next? It is important to have considered who your audience will be ahead of actually writing your novel. By

'Be sure that you've completed sufficient research and planning for you to feel confident that you can start writing a well-structured and thought out novel.'

considering who will read your book you'll be able to tailor the voice of either the lead character or you, the narrator, to the specific audience's needs. Furthermore, by identifying your audience you'll also be able to identify early on the specific genre that your story fits into, and the leading themes that your story should embrace to keep your audience interested as the novel progresses.

Now, you're ready to write!

Rewarding progress

'To keep you pressing forward with your writing and to keep your motivation levels high be sure to recognise what you've achieved so far, and to reward this achievement in a small way.'

It doesn't matter how committed you are to writing this novel or how much enthusiasm you have for your story, at some point during the writing process you'll need to give yourself a little boost to spur you on. We all feel deflated at times, or frustrated, or tired, or even overwhelmed by the magnitude of the task at hand. This is perfectly normal. To keep you pressing forward with your writing and to keep your motivation levels high be sure to recognise what you've achieved so far, and to reward this achievement in a small way.

We saw in chapter 2 the importance of setting yourself internal goals for the completion of your manuscript. As you reach each of these internal goals, reward your accomplishment in some way. It doesn't need to be a fancy reward each time. Buy yourself a nice coffee, cook your favourite meal, have a social drink, award yourself a lie-in! These small pleasures in life are the perfect indulgence to experience when celebrating a mini writing success. In return you'll find that you've a fresher mind and a more positive and creative approach to continuing with the next stage of your novel.

Coping with writer's block

Suffering? Writer's block can be as debilitating for a seasoned professional as a newly developing writer. In serious cases writers have been known to give up their chosen careers, in other cases, writing becomes a chore, or even a daunting experience.

If you find yourself suffering from writer's block, try not to panic. Following are some tips on how to accept that writer's block is an inevitable part of the writing process, and how to work through writer's block as quickly and painlessly as possible.

- Set aside time to write – Even if you suspect you may be wasting your time, make sure you have a schedule. Arrive at your chosen place, be it office, living room, café or park ready to write.

- Give yourself manageable tasks – Don't expect to write reams and reams in one sitting, you will only disappoint yourself. Instead be pleasantly surprised if you discover you have written more than 500 words! Don't be too hard on yourself if today you don't make your target, there's always tomorrow.

- Keep to deadlines – Despite my saying don't be too hard on yourself, try your best to keep to deadlines you have set, because getting behind will add stress you do not need. So the rule is allow time for error! Make sure that deadlines are realistic and give you a little extra time should you have difficulty.

- Be positive – Sounds easy, doesn't it? But a positive mental attitude can really affect your ability to write. Expecting that you will be able to make progress in your writing session can really aid you.

- Be patient – If it doesn't come straight away try some writing exercises based around your task. For example, if you're writing a piece of fiction, doodle your characters, their homes, their work space or friends. Even drawing will inspire your creative mood and enhance your knowledge of your characters, inspiring your writing. There are many 'self-help' books with writer's exercises. Get one; leave it on the book shelf or next to the desk, just in case you need a little creative pick-me-up!

- Examine why you have this particular problem – Is it that you just can't get down to it? You have creative issues? Is the space you are in not conducive to writing, could you relocate? Or is there a more serious problem you need to address? If it is the latter, you need to do everything you can to address the problem. Either write about your anxieties or talk through them with a friend. Often you will discover, although cliché, 'a problem shared is a problem halved'!

- Work more – Sounds crazy but often writers discover that they are unable to work on a particular task, but are able to work on another. By switching between the two they work through the writer's block.

- Think! Why are you doing this? – Remembering why you started your novel can help you overcome the difficulties you are experiencing with writer's block.

- Time off for good behaviour! – Just finished your last writing task? Take a well-earned break, ensuring you are refreshed for your next assignment.

- Don't give up – If you can't do it today, it's not the end of the world. Take your time, talk any problems through and remain calm.

'Remembering why you started your novel can help you overcome the difficulties you are experiencing with writer's block.'

Reviews, edits and rewrites

You've completed your story – congratulations! Don't, however, rush to send out your manuscript to welcoming publishers or literary agents just yet. Your novel has been drafted . . . it is not, however, complete.

As Wells (*Writing Non-Fiction Books: The Essential Guide*) states: 'Now comes the real hard work of authorship – converting your first draft into a saleable book'.

There are a number of ways to approach a review, edit and rewrite of your novel. The stages below represent perhaps the most commonly used approach. By completing each stage in turn, you can be sure that you'll have reviewed and finalised your manuscript in as thorough a way as possible.

1. Read through your drafted novel in its entirety. Use this read as an opportunity to get a sense of the story that you've created. Overall, are you happy with the way that the characters are represented? Do you find the plot intriguing? Do the subplots work? Does the diction flow? Is the conclusion satisfactory for the reader?

2. Identify any repetitions in your novel, either in terms of words used, phrases used or actions conveyed. It can be helpful to use the 'find' feature found in Microsoft Word software packages to identify words or phrases that you

use time and time again. Once identified, these words or phrases can be replaced with something new and fresh, and repetitions in action or storyline can be removed.

3. Next, taking each chapter at a time, read the text out loud. You can do this alone or with a person who you trust. How does the text sound? Are there any sections that are difficult to read, that don't flow well? Work on these sections by editing and rewriting parts of the text to enhance and ease the way the story is written.

4. Now look at the way that the text of each chapter appears on the page. Are there any paragraphs that are just a little too long? Do large paragraphs of text overshadow the dialogue? Is this deliberate? If not, how can you amend the content to better balance your writing?

5. Look at the metaphors you've used throughout your novel. Metaphors are of great literary use when it comes to describing objects, environments, people and situations. But they should be used with care – keep metaphors simple and be sure to not overuse them. As you review your novel, check that each metaphor is relevant and that it adds to the quality of your writing.

6. Check your novel for clichés. The odd cliché can be squeezed into a novel without anyone noticing too much. But too many clichés will frustrate the reader and will in turn detract from the overarching story you're trying to convey.

7. Finally, work through your manuscript with a fine-tooth comb, searching for grammar, spelling and punctuation errors. Better still, enlist the support of a proofreading company to complete this thorough trawl for you.

'Read through your drafted novel in its entirety. Use this read as an opportunity to get a sense of the story that you've created.'

Getting a second opinion

Once you've completed the drafting, revising, editing and finalising of your novel, you may choose to allow others to read your book before you send it out into the big wide world of publishing.

There are many benefits to having another individual read your book before you start searching for a publisher or literary agent. By enlisting another person to read through your story you'll be able to get their thoughts and ideas on how well the novel works; what they liked about the story and where they feel that the story could be enhanced, amended or expanded. You may choose to amend your novel further in light of their comments, or you may choose to retain the original text, but either way, their input will be valuable.

Generally, there are two choices when it comes to seeking a second opinion; ask a trusted friend or family member to read the text or use the services of a professional editorial company. Many writers find that the input received from professional editorial services is invaluable as they receive a non-biased response which is based on significant experience and creative writing knowledge. However, editorial companies can be expensive and so it may be more appropriate to ask friends to read your novel for you, remembering to insist that they are as critical as possible in order for their feedback to be of realistic value.

It can be scary putting the novel that you've spent so much time, energy and love on, out there for people to read and critically review. But remember that once the book is published there will be many, many people reading it and commenting upon the content. And so it is better to have external opinion provided about the novel before it is published, so that you have the opportunity to make any final revisions should you so wish.

'Many writers find that the input received from professional editorial services is invaluable as they receive a non-biased response which is based on significant experience and creative writing knowledge.'

Summing Up

- Committing your novel to paper is both scary and exhilarating. All of the preparation and research can finally come to fruition as you start to move your ideas on from the planning stage to the more concrete stage of chapter drafting and content writing.

- Writing a novel is often a long and laborious task that will require you to adhere as far as possible to your writing timetable and reward your achievements frequently to keep motivation levels high.

- Manage writer's block as efficiently and calmly as possible.

- Review, edit and revise your book a number of times in order to finalise the novel.

- Remember too that, once completed, the existence of your novel will represent a huge personal achievement for you, and one that you should be immensely proud of.

Chapter Eleven

Publishing Your Novel

It is an amazing feeling to have completed a novel – congratulations! There aren't that many people in the world who can say that they have written a novel so you should be very pleased with yourself. Now is the time to celebrate and allow yourself to be proud of what you've accomplished. Go out for dinner or for a drink with family members or friends; take a day and treat yourself by partaking in a little bit of shopping; sit and read; watch a sports match; have afternoon tea and cake – whatever takes your fancy!

Once the novel is complete, and you feel that you've sufficiently enjoyed the celebrations, the next step is to think about publishing your novel, and getting it out there in the wider world for other people to read and enjoy.

Unfortunately, for many people it can be tricky and time-consuming to secure a publishing deal with a publishing house. The larger, well-established publishing houses will often only accept manuscripts from literary agents, and so as a new writer this means that you need to successfully locate yourself an agent in order to have a shot at striking a deal with a large or international publisher. And agents aren't easy to locate either. Most are already full to capacity and will therefore simply refuse you because they don't have space to take on another writer; others have a very tight acceptance criterion. Furthermore, literary agencies will also take a percentage cut of any royalties made by your novel once it has been published. So brace yourself, the road to publication is often long and frustrating.

However, over the last decade the publishing industry has seen a huge boom in the number of books that are self-published and in the number of books that have been created as e-books. These options are now accessible, and in many cases, affordable alternatives to the traditional approach of submitting your manuscript to publishing houses or literary agencies and waiting months at a time to receive a response to your submission.

'Brace yourself, the road to publication is often long and frustrating.'

Self publishing

Self publishing was once known as 'vanity publishing', so called because it was perceived to be a publication route that 'failed' authors used when they couldn't rid themselves of that burning desire to see their manuscript turned into a hardback. In recent years however, as the number of fiction pieces taken on by traditional publishers has dwindled, self publishing has become a fantastic route for good writers to get their work printed, showcased and sold.

Self publishing itself attracts a number of pros and cons. On the plus side it is accessible – there are a number of well-renowned self-publishing houses out there. It is a quick and relatively pain-free way of getting your book printed, you can often have total control of how the book looks and feels, and a wide number of self-publishing companies now also have marketing arms attached to them to support the ongoing advertising and sales of your book. On the other hand, if you opt for a self-publishing route you'll find that you have to do a lot of work yourself to get your book out there on the shelves of local or national bookshops, you have to take full responsibility for proofreading and editing the manuscript before it goes to print, and you do have to pay for your book to be published, and then often again for each copy of the book you want.

'If you opt for a self-publishing route you'll find that you have to do a lot of work yourself to get your book out there on the shelves of local or national bookshops.'

Different methods of publishing

Therefore, as you start to think about getting your novel published, the first thing you need to do is assess which publishing route is best for you. The list of questions in the following table should help you begin to determine whether your novel is best suited to:

- A traditional publisher approach.
- An approach via a literary agency.
- Self publication.
- Electronic publication (via an e-book).

Deciding upon a publication route

Answer each of the quiz style questions below to determine the most appropriate publication route for your novel:

Question No.	Question	Very important	Quite important	Not too concerned	Not important
1.	How important is it for you to physically hold a copy of your printed novel?				
2.	Is it important that your novel is printed by a specific publishing house?				
3.	How important is it that you earn money by selling your novel?				
4.	How important is it that you see your book in bookstores?				
5.	Is it important to you to have a big launch for the release of your book?				

Question No.	Question	Very important	Quite important	Not too concerned	Not important
6.	Is it important to you to see your book well marketed?				
7.	How important is it that you have a wide audience of individuals who can purchase your book?				
8.	How important is it that your book reaches a younger audience?				
9.	Is it important to you that your book is thought of as 'embracing' contemporary technology?				
10.	Is it important that your book drives lots of sales?				

Your answers to these questions will help determine how important it is for you to pursue a traditional publishing route, either by approaching a publisher directly or by securing a relationship with a literary agency and letting the agency approach the publishers on your behalf.

If you have answered 'Very important', or 'Quite important' to questions 2, 3, 4, 6 and 10, then pursuing a traditional publishing route initially would be the best option for you.

If, however, you have answered 'Not too concerned' or 'Not important' to questions 2, 3, 4, 6 and 10, then you are more flexible about the publishing route you take, and could find that a self-publishing route or even the publication of your book as an e-book would work perfectly well for you. In addition, if you have answered 'Very important' or 'Quite important' to questions 7, 8, and 9 then you should strongly consider opting for an e-book publication.

Identifying relevant publishers

Regardless of which publication route you choose to take, you will need to draw up a list of publishers or agencies which can potentially fulfil your publication needs.

If you are opting for a traditional publisher approach you will need to create a list of publishers who are currently accepting unsolicited fiction manuscripts.

If you are opting to first align yourself with a literary agent you will need to create a list of agencies who are currently accepting new fiction authors.

If you are opting for a self-publishing route you will need to create a list of self-publishing companies who publish fiction, can cope with the specifics of your book (i.e. the use of colour or imagery) and who fall within your price range.

If you are opting for an e-book route you will need to create a list of publishers who create e-books.

'One of the best places to start to pull together a list of suitable publishers or literary agents is by looking through the latest *Writers' and Artists' Yearbook.*'

How to find publishers and literary agents

One of the best places to start to pull together a list of suitable publishers or literary agents is by looking through the latest *Writers' and Artists' Yearbook*. This chunky reference book can be purchased from all good bookshops, and can also be found in libraries. A version of the yearbook can be found online too (see the help list).

The *Writers' and Artists' Yearbook* lists all of the main publishers and agents in the UK and Ireland, and those that are overseas. There are two separate lists for publishers and agencies, and each list is provided in alphabetical order. The details of the publishing house or literary agency provided are concise, but they provide everything you need to know. Under many of the entries you'll find the following information:

- Company name.
- Company contact details – address, fax and telephone numbers, email address, etc.
- The name of the publishing lead at the company.
- What sort of books they publish or represent.
- Whether or not they accept unsolicited manuscripts
- Whether or not they produce e-books.
- Whether or not they have an associated self-publishing arm or if they purely work with self-publishing novels.

Using this information, you can create a list of suitable publishers or literary agencies to approach.

Writing magazines and writing websites are also very useful when it comes to locating a suitable publisher or agent (see the help list). Publications such as *Writers' Forum, The Writing Magazine* or *Writing News* all contain advertisements from publishers and agents, and are a particularly good place to look for recommended self-publishing and e-publishing bodies. *Writing News* is a monthly publication that provides almost one hundred news stories relating to the writing world. A large number of these news items alert readers to traditional publishers who are, at that point in time, accepting unsolicited manuscripts. This is therefore an extremely handy resource for individuals who have opted for a traditional publisher approach.

Approaching a publisher

How you approach a publisher will depend upon which publication route you have chosen to take.

If you are opting for a traditional publisher approach or to align yourself with a literary agent you will need to create a submission pack, which will include a synopsis of your manuscript, a selection of sample chapters from your manuscript, your biography and a well-written cover letter.

If you are opting for a self-publishing route you will be purchasing a service from the publishing company and so you should not be required to provide material to the publishing company in order to secure a contract. However, often the self-publishing company will want to review your manuscript first, to ensure that it doesn't contain any inappropriate material.

If you are opting for an e-book route, again as you are likely to be purchasing this service from the publishing company you should not be required to provide material to the publishing company in order to secure a contract. As with the self-publishing route, you may be required to submit your manuscript for an initial review, so that the publishing company can satisfy themselves that the book does not contain any inappropriate material.

'It is important that you follow the style and submission guidelines that each publishing house or literary agency holds.'

Creating a submission pack

Once you have your list of publishers or agents to whom you are going to submit your manuscript, you can start to pull together your book proposal submission – the submission pack.

Publishers and agents often have very strict rules regarding what book proposal submissions should look like. They will normally have their own style guidelines that they like submissions to follow; these usually relate to font size and style, line and paragraph spacing and word counts. Each publishing company or literary agency will also specify what particular information they want you to include within your submission pack. Some, for example, may want you to include market research regarding the potential audience of your manuscript. Others may ask you to state why you feel your manuscript 'fits' with their current publication list.

It is important that you follow the style and submission guidelines that each publishing house or literary agency holds. Publishers and agents receive hundreds of unsolicited manuscripts each day, and they can easily disregard yours immediately if they can see that you haven't abided by their submission rules. To ensure that you know the different style and submission guidelines for each of your chosen publishers or agents, try to locate the 'submissions' section on their website or call their main office number and ask for their submission criteria to be posted or emailed to you.

It is helpful to keep all of the submission information and style guidelines for the publishers and/or agents you've chosen to submit to in one place. A good way to do this is to draw up a table where you can easily hold this information, and access it each time you need it. The template below can be used as an example:

Name of publisher/agency	Specific style guidelines	Specific submission guidelines
Beacon Press	Double spacing, Arial font, size 12 throughout.	Submit an author biography, synopsis and three sample chapters.
S.B. Publications	Double spacing, minimum of size 12 throughout, do not underline any text.	Submit a cover letter, synopsis and two sample chapters.

In general, you'll find that most publishers and agents require you to use a minimum of 1.5 line spacing and to use a font that is easy to read and is in size 12. You'll also find that almost all publishers and agents will request 4 basic documents as part of your submission pack. These are:

■ A cover letter.

- A synopsis of your manuscript.

- A couple of sample chapters from your manuscript.

- An author biography.

The following table highlights the principle 'dos' and 'don'ts' of producing these four documents. Try to keep them in mind when pulling your submission packs together.

Submission Pack Document	Do!	Don't!
The cover letter	▪ Keep it to one A4 page. ▪ Address the letter to the appropriate editor for your manuscript genre. ▪ State in the letter why you are approaching them as a publisher/agency. Explain how your manuscript fits with the books they currently publish or the authors they currently represent. ▪ State why you think this story would sell well now, in today's society/market. ▪ Be professional in your tone and writing style. ▪ Check for grammar and spelling errors.	▪ Forget to address the letter correctly. A 'Dear Sir/Madam' will not suffice. ▪ Offer your opinion or anyone else's opinion on the book. The only opinion that matters to the editor or agent is their own. ▪ Tell the editor or agent how he/she is going to feel once they have read the book – let them make up their own mind.

Submission Pack Document	Do!	Don't!
The synopsis	▪ Remember that your synopsis should be a précis of the entire manuscript. That includes the ending! ▪ Write the synopsis in the present tense. ▪ Detail briefly the main plot and any key scenes. ▪ Make it obvious who the main character is, what their ultimate goal is, and who or what stands between them and their goal.	▪ Let the synopsis be too long. Two A4 pages should be your word count aim. ▪ Conceal the ending. This will only frustrate the editor or agent and is a telling sign of a novice writer. ▪ Leave any poor spelling or grammar errors.
The sample chapters	▪ Choose your favourite chapters as they probably include some of your best writing. ▪ Choose at least one chapter from the beginning of the novel. ▪ Make sure these chapters are as well written as possible.	▪ Submit more than approximately 50 manuscript pages for your sample chapters. ▪ Forget to do a final check through of these chapters to ensure that the spelling, grammar and punctuation is squeaky clean.

Submission Pack Document	Do!	Don't!
The author biography	▪ Keep it succinct and to the point. ▪ Include information about previous writing successes or publications. ▪ Include anything that makes you or your life intriguing or particularly interesting, and thus saleable for a publisher or agent.	▪ Create a biography that is over one A4 page in length.

A burning question that enters all writers' minds at some point during the manuscript submission process is 'Can I submit a submission pack to more than one literary agency or publishing house at a time?' The answer nowadays is 'Yes'. Publishers and agents alike expect authors to submit their manuscript to several other companies at the same time, and it is acceptable to do so, as long as the publishing house or literary agency hasn't specified that they do not accept multiple submissions.

And finally, remember to include a stamped, self-addressed envelope with each submission pack you send out.

Summing Up

- The 4 most popular ways of publishing a novel are (1) via a traditional publisher, (2) via a literary agent, (3) by self publishing, or (4) by creating an e-book.

- There are pros and cons to self publication, and you should assess these before embarking on the self publication of your novel.

- There are lots of tools out there to help you decide which publishers or agents you want to approach regarding the publication of your novel.

- Once you have decided which publishers or agents to approach; be sure to obtain details of their individual style guidelines and submission criteria.

- A submission pack usually needs to include a cover letter, a synopsis, a selection of sample chapters and an author biography.

- A cover letter should be addressed to an appropriate contact.

- A synopsis should précis the entire manuscript, including the ending!

- At least one sample chapter should come from the beginning of your manuscript.

- Your author's biography should include information about what makes you stand out from the crowd.

Help List

Book distributors

Amazon
Web: www.services.amazon.co.uk
Email: Via an online form through the webpage: services.amazon.co.uk/
standards/contact-us/

Bertrams
Web: www.bertrams.com
Email: books@bertrams.com
Tel: 0871 803 6600

Gardners
Web: www.gardners.com
Email: sph@gardners.com
Tel: 01323 521444

Nielsen
Nielsen House
London Road
Headington
Oxford
Oxfordshire
OX3 9RX
Web: www.nielsen.com/UK
Tel: 01865 742742

Marketing resources

www.venuefinder.com
www.writers-circles.com/circles
www.press-release-writing.com

www.pressbox.co.uk (a free press release distribution site)

Photography libraries
www.istockphoto.com
www.gettyimages.co.uk

Useful books

Gotham Writers' Workshop: Writing Fiction
A & C Black, London
www.acblack.com

Writers' and Artists' Yearbook (annual)
A & C Black, London
www.writersandartists.co.uk

The Writer's Handbook (annual)
By Barry Turner (ed), Macmillan, Hampshire
www.thewritershandbook.com

Writers' Market (annual)
By David & Charles, Devon
www.writersmarket.com

Useful magazines

The Self Publishing Magazine
Troubadour Publishing Ltd.
9 Priory Business Park
Wistow Road
Kibworth Beauchamp
Leicestershire LE8 0RX
Web: www.selfpublishingmagazine.co.uk

Writers' Forum

PO Box 6337
Bournemouth BH1 9EH
Web: www.writers-forum.com

Writers Online

Warners Group Publications plc
5th Floor
31-32 Park Row
Leeds
LS1 5JD
Web: www.writersonline.co.uk
Tel: 0113 200 2929

Useful organisations

Authors' Licensing and Collecting Society Ltd (ALCS)

The Writer's House
13 Haydon Street
London EC3 1DB
Web: www.alcs.co.uk
Tel: 020 7264 5700

The Independent Publishers' Guild

PO Box 12
Llain
Login SA34 0WU
Web: www.ipg.uk.com
Email: info@ipg.uk.com
Tel: 01437 563335

Society for Editors and Proofreaders (SfEP)

Aspley House
176 Upper Richmond Rd
Putney
London SW15 2SH
Tel: 020 8785 6155
Web: www.sfep.org.uk
Email: administrator@sfep.org.uk

The Society of Authors

The Society of Authors
84 Drayton Gardens
London SW10 9SB
Web: www.societyofauthors.org
Email: info@societyofauthors.org
Tel: 0207 3736642

The Society of Indexers

Woodbourn Business Centre
10 Jessell Street
Sheffield S9 3HY
Web: www.indexers.org.uk
Email: admin@indexers.org.uk
Tel: 0114 244 9561